Climate Machines, Fascist Drives, and Truth

Climate Machines
Fascist Drives
and Truth

WILLIAM E. CONNOLLY

Duke University Press | *Durham and London* | 2019

Printed in the United States of America
on acid-free paper ∞
Designed by Matthew Tauch
Typeset in Whitman and Helvetica Neue LT Std
by Westchester Publishing Services
Library of Congress Cataloging-in-Publication Data
Names: Connolly, William E., [date] author.
Title: Climate machines, fascist drives, and truth /
William E. Connolly.
Description: Durham : Duke University Press, 2019. |
Includes bibliographical references and index.
Identifiers: LCCN 2019008725 (print)
LCCN 2019016269 (ebook)
ISBN 9781478007258 (ebook)
ISBN 9781478005896 (hardcover : alk. paper)
ISBN 9781478006558 (pbk. : alk. paper)
Subjects: LCSH: Global environmental change—Philosophy. |
Climatic changes—Philosophy. | Global environmental
change—Political aspects. | Capitalism—Philosophy. |
Truth—Philosophy.
Classification: LCC GE149 (ebook) | LCC GE149 .c665 2019
(print) | DDC 304.2/8—dc23
LC record available at https://lccn.loc.gov/2019008725

Contents

Acknowledgments

I would like to thank Tom Dumm, Stephanie Erev, Jairus Grove, Anatoli Ignatov, Franziska Strack, Nidesh Lawtoo, Bonnie Honig, Libby Anker, Lars Tonder, Catherine Keller, Nils Kupzok, Nicole Grove, Tvrtko Vrdjolak, Anand Pandian, Naveeda Khan, and Alex Livingston for their comments on earlier drafts of these essays, as they were being prepared and revised.

Franziska Strack did double duty, proposing helpful changes in the essays as she also prepared the index and bibliography.

The second essay was presented to the Deleuze and Guattari Studies Conference in July 2019 at Royal Holloway, University of London, and to the Western Political Science Association in San Diego in April 2019. I appreciate the thoughts advanced by participants in those discussions.

I also appreciate very much the advice and counsel of Courtney Berger as she saw yet another Duke project through its various phases. Jane Bennett, once again, read these essays in their early stages and communed with me often as we thought about the title, themes, and format together. I am fortunate to be related to her as a writer, interlocutor, and comrade in arms.

Introduction

Climate, Fascism, Truth

Donald Trump came to power not only by attacking precarious minorities, pushing white triumphalism, slamming the media, courting white
evangelicals, demeaning democratic allies of America, pushing misogyny,
conspiring with Putin, talking endlessly about a territorial wall, and promising battered workers a return to an old manufacturing regime. He also
ridiculed warnings about climate change. These themes do not fit together
into a necessary combination, but they do slide into a convenient, politi-
cally potent package. One way to court a deindustrialized white working
and lower middle class—especially those in "flyover zones" between the
two coasts—is to promise that you will bring back the old industrial world
by returning to the coal, oil, car, steel, truck, labor, race, highway, and
gasoline regime that was in place during a golden age.

The golden years were the 1950s and early 1960s. That is why the nos-
talgic word "again" is so crucial on the Trump red hat. It incites prejudices
and support for simple solutions among a neglected white working and
lower middle class caught between the income/wealth concentration machine of the neoliberal right and the noble movements of the pluralizing

left. This seething constituency has faced disrespect, wage stagnation, job insecurity, weakened labor unions, a very expensive social infrastructure of consumption, underwater mortgages created by a neoliberal meltdown, underfunded schools, difficulty in sending its kids to increasingly expensive colleges, high medical costs, and insecure retirement prospects.[1] Their condition is not as bad as that of the urban and rural poor, but it is severe enough. It is a constituency simmering with ambivalences that Trump strives to pull in a destructive direction.

Many people in Europe and America worried about the environment in the 1950s and '60s. But there were few significant clarion calls about the multiple dangers and deleterious effects of rapid climate change, even though such forces were well underway below the radar of global attention. The most vibrant social movements—on behalf of racial equality, feminism, gay rights, the New Left, antiwar protests, and environmentalism— had not yet lifted off either in the United States or in Europe. "Make America Great Again" refers to a mythic age tied to forgetting (or worse) its terrible injuries; injuries embodied in Jim Crow, antigay actions, misogyny, and McCarthyism. Cruelty, denialism, and an accusatory culture are central to Trumpism. Cruel acceptance of suffering spawned by racism, misogyny, environmental destruction, and empire joined with denial that another massive bill is coming due with respect to galloping climate change.

The Trump syndrome is not only destructive because it refuses to address serious injuries and profound issues. It is also dangerous because, as the climate bills become increasingly palpable, fascist temptations will intensify among many whose current denials become more difficult to sustain.

I

This is not a book only about the dangers and strategies of fascism, however. I wrote a book about that recently.[2] This study consists of three essays about how galloping planetary climate change works; the challenges it poses to dominant images of the subject, capitalism, nature, theology, truth, and governance; and the regimes of truth that delayed the earth sciences, the humanities, the social sciences, and democratic citizens (in roughly that order) from responding to these processes in a more timely way, particularly in the United States. The essays turn to the dangers of fascism from time to time because of the gap that yawns between the radical shifts in perspective needed to respond to the climate machine and fascist reactions that grow more tempting as the accelerating pace of that time machine becomes too palpable to evade.

The first essay focuses on three thinkers—Sophocles, Mary Shelley, and Bernard Williams. Writing in different times and places, they advanced overlapping insights that, had they been widely taken up in major Eurocentric theories, may well have advanced understandings sooner about the unruliness of this planet. Sophocles—through the vehicle of the gods—appreciated how periodic eruptions of plagues, earthquakes, volcanoes, and raging seas bounce into the fabric of social life and civic spirituality. His tragedies would be mere exercises in cultural internalism if those volatilities were subtracted from them.

Mary Shelley, writing in the early 1800s after experiencing a mysterious year without a summer in Europe, populates her great novel *Frankenstein: Prometheus Unbound* with radical shifts in terrain, changing weather systems, thoughts about evolution, the dangers of scientific hubris, and hints about the partially self-organizing trajectories of planetary systems.

Bernard Williams, indebted to Sophocles and writing late in the twentieth century, strives to insert the image of an unruly nonhuman world into the center of thought. In his own way, he sought to fold insights from a minor tradition of Euro-American thought into the contours of analytic philosophy. That endeavor did not succeed at the time.

A counterfactual question is posed in the first essay: What would (or might) have happened to the earth sciences, the humanities, and the social sciences in Euro-America if—rather than being transfixed by themes, philosophies, and divine theologies that treat the earth as a set of glacial regularities that change very slowly—important voices in those domains had drawn inspiration from thinkers such as Sophocles and Shelley? Indeed, how much earlier might the galloping processes of planetary climate change have been diagnosed if more modern thinkers had drawn from figures in the minor tradition of European thought such as Hesiod, Sophocles, Heraclitus, Lucretius, Duns Scotus, Spinoza, Kropotkin, and Nietzsche to challenge some assumptions made by figures in the major tradition, figures ranging from Plato, Aristotle, Augustine, and Aquinas to Kant, Hegel, Weber, Hayek, Arendt, and Rawls?[3] How much sooner would earth scientists, humanists, and larger populations have come to appreciate the periodic volatility of earth processes, especially (but not only) when those systems are joined to the depredations of extractive capitalism, socialism, and communism, if early thinkers on the minor list had been consulted earlier, more generally, and more closely?

The question is impossible to answer with confidence. But posing it may help us to discern how deeply a series of intellectual, existential, economic, and political pressures still bear down on many in these domains. It might, to use a phrase summoned from Foucault in the last essay, help us to press more powerfully upon "regimes of truth" that remain powerful today.

So let us distinguish roughly—even crudely—between two European traditions, each full of its own internal debates. The first seeks (and usually claims to secure) strong anchors for its thought while the second often tends to be more speculative and pluralistic. The first tends to forge sharp distinctions between nature and culture while the second tends to emphasize their imbrications. The first often supports a morality of either transcendent command or transcendental derivation while the second often pursues an ethic of cultivation in which people work upon themselves to strengthen contingent seeds of presumptive generosity if and when they already find some expression: the second thus emphasizes the interconnections between how you think, feel, and live. The first tends to set cultural study within the assumption of long-term planetary gradualism while the second often tends to challenge that very idea. And so forth.[4]

Certainly, within the major tradition there are fundamental debates. Kant and Augustine differ on the relation to God pious ones must assume, though the defining characteristics of the omnipotent God each pursues are eerily similar by comparison to discussions of divinity in Hesiod, Sophocles, Epicurus, Spinoza, and Whitehead. Augustine treats an omnipotent, personal God as an essential article of faith; Kant treats it as a necessary postulate of human moral existence as such. Weber, Hayek, and Rawls differ critically on the defining characteristics of capitalism and possible alternatives to it. Marx straddles the major and minor traditions, at once challenging transcendent claims and embracing an assumption of planetary gradualism this study seeks to explode. In the latter respect he deviated from the thought of the radical anarchist and climate scientist Prince Kropotkin, who preceded him. Arendt explores the politics of creative enactment in ways that distinguish her from several others on the list, but she retains a strict nature/culture division.

Debates within the major tradition are thus multiple and important. But the major debates also tend to drain attention from how the debating partners often converge in downplaying historic periods of volatility in partially self-organizing planetary processes such as climate, polar glacier flows, volcanoes, drought systems, monsoons, mountain glacier transitions, El Niños, and the ocean conveyor system. They too often assume planetary gradualism, a gradualism in which even the sudden eruption of a massive volcano or a major asteroid hit is said to be followed by the slow return to a planet of long, slow cycles.

I teach several major European thinkers regularly, to discern the putative grounds of their systems, to see how they argue, to probe how their rhetorical styles filter into their arguments, to explore issues between them, to uncover the tacit background of contemporary debates, to gain insights about connections between spiritual, economic, ethical, and political forces, and to identify internal flashpoints from which one could launch a different journey from the dominant theme this or that thinker actually forged. For there are often discernible minor themes in them, themes noted but less often pursued by the authors. Such subordinate themes open doors to forge potential and creative intersections between major and minor thinkers.[5] The major thinkers, then, are full of riches.

But Sophocles, Shelley, and Williams express tendencies more widely distributed in the minor tradition. By exploring themes and existential concerns each projects, we may gain a preliminary sense of how long minor thinkers have sensed planetary volatilities muted by the major tradition—either through denial or by locating observed volatilities in a rift for which humans are primordially responsible. The first essay, after reviewing how Williams strives to think anew with Sophocles and Thucydides, explores how Sophocles bumps unruly nonhuman events into key turns in his human dramas. We then repeat another version of that story through an engagement with Mary Shelley.

The first essay closes with a critique of what I call sociocentrism. It is joined to a corollary charge to fold nonhuman, planetary processes more intimately into the humanities and human sciences. Sociocentrism is the tacit idea that one set of social processes and changes can be explained (or, in some of its versions, interpreted) almost solely by reference to more fundamental social processes. The nineteenth- and twentieth-century doctrines of gradualism in the earth and human sciences themselves—the assumption about planetary processes that tacitly supports sociocentrism in the humanities and was not dismantled in the earth sciences until the 1980s—must be displaced today within the humanities too in order to come to terms with the dynamics and consequences of the contemporary climate machine.

Some people will say that this or that major thinker anticipated the story of an unruly planet. Some did, albeit often in dark ways. Weber worried about what would happen to capitalism when the last ton of coal is burned. Marx, the straddler, attended to connections between specific natural resources deployed in historic regimes—water mills, wood, coal, or steam, for instance—and particular relations of production. Marx and Engels also appreciated how European deforestation promoted drought.[6] But none of these thinkers attended to how volatile planetary processes, with self-organizing powers of their own, roll back and forth with social and political forces to form time machines that periodically change rapidly and are irreducible to either social forms or nonhuman processes taken alone. The first essay seeks to render the humanities and the human sciences highly receptive to such detailed engagements.

II

The second essay takes the leap. Expressing one debt to a revolution in the earth sciences launched in the 1980s and another to a recent analysis by two thinkers in the minor tradition. I draw upon Deleuze and Guattari in *A Thousand Plateaus* to outline the Anthropocene as an abstract, planetary time machine. To provide preliminary orientation, an abstract machine is a partially self-organizing cluster of heterogeneous forces and agencies that feed upon and fuel each other, often accelerating as the diverse components become more densely imbricated. Reader alert: such a temporal machine is neither a mechanism nor an organism. It is not reducible to human agencies taken alone, nor do the diverse forces and agencies that compose it always follow a slow, regular trajectory. It might move slowly along one trajectory for a long time and then take a sharp turn. Sometimes the turn is rapid, as when an asteroid strike in Mexico and a volcanic eruption in India extinguished dinosaurs and 50 percent of species life, setting the stage for a new turn in evolution, or when the ocean conveyor system, pulling warm weather into Europe and the eastern seaboard of America, seems to have crashed to a rapid halt 12,700 years ago, changing climate rapidly when it closed down. Or consider how the Holocene itself—the roughly eleven-thousand-year period during which agriculture was initiated and human population growth accelerated—may have stuttered into place during a ten-year period.[7]

We do not inhabit a world composed of homogeneous connections alone; connections are also forged between heterogeneous entities—such as wasps and orchids, gut bacteria and human moods, ticks and human disease, CO_2 emissions and ocean algae growth, and the horizontal transfer of genetic material into humans and other species through viral infusions. The climate machine of the Anthropocene draws into its orbit heterogeneous agencies and forces as it unleashes highly asymmetrical effects upon diverse human and nonhuman populations around the globe.

Let us call an *agent* any entity that can strive or pursue a purpose, however simple. A *force* is an entity on the move without purpose, capable of impinging upon or ingressing into other forces and agencies. Glaciers, tectonic plates, and carcinogens are forces. Bacteria, fleas, rats, and human beings are agents, with varying degrees and types of capacity. Bacteria, rats, and humans also possess both individual and collective capacities of agency, as exemplified by those quorum calls of bacteria in the human gut and by organized social movements. The diverse agencies and forces composing the climate machine of today include, for starters, extractive capitalism, several democratic constituencies whose identities and interests are tied to carbon extraction, CO_2 atmospheric emissions, polar glacier melts with self-amplifying powers, growing regions of drought that recoil back on populations, deforestation which feeds upon itself, ocean acidification, refugee pressures flowing from hard-hit subtropical regions to temporal regions, potential monsoon interruptions, social movements to combat these pressures, and neofascist reactions in old capitalist states upon such diverse, interactive processes. The *triggers* pulled by extractive capitalism are exceeded by numerous planetary *amplifiers* they set into motion. And the latter recoil back on both those systems and upon undercapitalized regions.

The second essay, after gauging shifting components in the current planetary machine and the regional asymmetry of its effects, turns to the danger of fascism in old capitalist states. The problem with accelerationist critiques of capitalism—which call upon the left to exacerbate the contradictions of capitalism until the system collapses and a new one can be built—is that they have not taken an adequate measure of the fascist danger residing precisely in such pressures. It would be better, I wager, if cross-regional constituencies mobilize internal and external pressures upon capitalist states at the same time, pressing them to introduce a series of rapid interim changes in the structure of investment, the infrastructure of consumption, state priorities of regulation, regional mitigation and reparation payments, and the spiritual ethos of the day. You can call such an agenda an improbable necessity of late modern times.

After exploring how capitalist institutions and spiritual energies help to constitute one another, I also hesitate over the temptation to call this latest climate machine "the Capitalocene." While appreciating contributions post-Marxist accounts make in grasping the critical role of capitalism in creating and sustaining the Anthropocene, the essay draws upon Kyle Harper's recent account in *The Fate of Rome* on the role of climate change and plagues during the fall of Rome to suggest that the contemporary issues are not reducible to capitalism alone. The fall of Rome was partly induced by the empire's imbrications with a larger climate machine of its own day, one that it both fed in some ways and was infected by in others. You could also explore the spiraling relations in precapitalist Europe between radical deforestation projects and the Medieval Warm Period.

Extractive capitalism—in its diverse modes—has become a more radical geological force today than any of its cultural predecessors. But attention to previous planetary volatilities helps us to gauge the amplifiers set into motion today and to think about possible responses to those conditions. Several contemporary amplifiers are identified until it becomes clear how and why the assumption of emission/climate parallelism is false. Parallelism, in this context, is the assumption that emissions and climate move along parallel tracks, so that an increase in the volume of the first will be matched by an increase in the temperature of the second, and so that a decline in emissions will produce a parallel decline in temperature. The introduction of amplifiers blows climate parallelism out of the water.

It is certainly imperative today to rethink and revise old capitalist practices and ideals of extraction, investment, the state, inequality, consumption, and growth—Keynesianism, social democracy, liberal schemes of rights and growth, neoliberalism, and fascist capitalism among them. Such projects are critical. But it may also be important to reconfigure several nineteenth- and twentieth-century ideals that have contended against capitalism. One danger of fascism today resides in the fact that, while extractive capitalism hurtles down its destructive course, several nineteenth-and twentieth-century ideals previously marshaled against it have lost much of their credibility too. The fictive myth of a radical return to the good old days—that is, the prototype fascist recipe of return to a mythic past— flourishes during a period of deindustrialization, climate stress, pressure on diverse regional populations, urgent refugee drives, and the faltering credibility of dominant social ideals that have contended against capitalism. I do not pursue that latter task closely in these essays, though the outlines of an approach are suggested.[8] An initial task, during an era haunted by the specter of fascism, is to show how the dynamics of the climate machine make it urgent to do so.

III

Well, this little study now arrives at a new flashpoint. It could explore a set of political strategies to respond democratically to the planetary climate machine. It could discuss more closely interim policy changes needed to turn capitalism in a new direction, a direction that could set the stage to move beyond capitalism. Those two issues, indeed, are crucial. But in the company of others I have pursued each of those tasks as extensively as I am now capable of doing in recent books. Indeed, I hope these essays will be placed into conversation with three recent books of mine, *Capitalism and Christianity, American Style* (2008), *Facing the Planetary* (2017), and *Aspirational Fascism* (2017). The first proposes a list of interim changes to American capitalism to promote a more ecological, egalitarian order and to fend off the danger of fascism. The second criticizes different versions of sociocentrism in radical, liberal, and neoliberal traditions, as it supports a cross-regional politics of swarming to reshape hegemonic practices in the domains of extraction, public investment, the infrastructure of consumption, the provision of public nets, regional mitigation and reparation payments, and the mobilization of social desire. The third charts Trumpism as a fascist agenda to exploit current stresses in the United States; it pursues an ideal of multifaceted, pluralizing, and egalitarian democracy to press against that danger.

So the third essay in this study takes another turn, one also linked to the first two essays. It draws upon two additional and recent thinkers in the minor tradition—Michel Foucault and Alfred North Whitehead—to pursue its task. It asks, how can the aspiration to truth by critical thinkers be preserved and refined as we come to terms with a world in which several unconscious habits of thought have become shaky?

Some commentators today link what they (crudely) call postmodernism to the deployment of "fake news" under Trumpism.[9] In doing so, they hope to kill two birds with one stone: rid the world of Trump and degrade critical perspectives that challenge the correspondence model of truth and neopositivist images of science.[10] Indeed, they sometimes seek to protect a regime of science that helped to secure the notion of planetary gradualism for centuries. I recently responded to such false equations in a preliminary post on *The Contemporary Condition*.[11] The task now is to extend and deepen the response.

The first thing to say about the equation between fake news and postmodernism is that it does not articulate the profound difference between parties who base their claims upon publicly available evidence and those who manufacture stories to incite racism, and so on. I am not a postmodernist so described: I believe in evidence-based claims, advance a positive ideal of democracy, and pursue a positive ethos of eco-egalitarian pluralism. And as far as I know, no postmodernist claimed that Iraq invaded the United States (rather than the other way around) or that weapons of mass destruction were found during that disastrous invasion.

To support evidence-based claims, however, does not mean that you think every issue is readily decided by recourse to facts currently available. Several issues on the cutting edges of evolutionary biology, quantum physics, climate science, neuroscience, political theory, and sociology today are replete with speculation and controversy. Their reasonable resolution often awaits the introduction of new concepts and theories, new testing devices, adjustment in subjective sensitivities to the world, access to evidence made available through those shifts, and shifts in metaphysical assumptions. The charge of a post-truth image of the world often discounts the importance of such adjustments in order to anchor itself in an image of sharp separation between facts and theories; it also denies the current relevance of metaphysical speculation. The historic shifts in thought between Aristotle, Descartes, Newton, Kant, Einstein, and Whitehead already suggest how much forgetting is embedded in such presumptions.

Second, it is important to attend to fundamental differences in affective tone and purpose that inform fascists and their democratic critics. As I say in "Fake News and 'Postmodernism,'"

> Fascists assert Big Lies dogmatically and rancorously to smear opponents and to gain authoritarian power so that only the ruler's word becomes legitimate; postmodernists—who often deny our ability to reduce competing metaphysical interpretations to one candidate alone—typically probe alternative interpretations to open a plurality of views for wider consideration. This fundamental difference between one ethos of dogmatism and another of presumptive generosity [to diverse constituencies and perspectives] is, of course, not noted by accusers. Perhaps . . . [neopositivists] who seek to pin the blame for fake news on postmodernism often themselves fail to note how differences in ethos or sensibility make a difference to both public culture and political inquiry.

A third area of debate between neopositivists and process theorists (as I call myself) who resist both fascism and neopositivism is more difficult to state briefly. But neopositivists often support a correspondence theory of truth and deny that the universe contains intersecting entities and processes sometimes marked by pulses of real creativity. They thus support a linear image of time. Process thinkers—embodying one modern outgrowth of the minor tradition—emphasize how multitemporal processes shape a world that periodically morphs in this or that way. We speculate, with evidential support, that knots of real creativity periodically populate aspects of the world, helping to change its direction. That means that explanation and interpretation are often inherently incomplete to themselves, not merely because of limited evidence but also because of creative intersections that bring novelty into the world.[12] We adopt a modified coherence vision of truth in order to examine such possibilities about the world and the shaky place of human beings and other species in it.

The recent blog post closes with the following statement:

A credible case can be made that sometimes something new emerges out of resonances back and forth between a cloudy fork from the past that was not taken and a current encounter. Such a speculative philosophy can be contested, of course. Nonetheless, the case for real creativity it sustains speaks to the artistic and aesthetic dimensions of life without either reducing everything to mere subjective constitution or flattening objectivity into the barren worlds of positivism and rational choice theory. All three of the latter traditions fail to appreciate the complexity and wonder of the world.[13]

IV

Such responses merely provide a promissory note, however. If a correspondence theory of truth—roughly, the contention that a proposition is true to the extent it correctly represents the character of the determinate objects studied—has fallen upon hard times, and if the celebration of a post-truth world is unnecessary and dangerous, how can process and minor theorists negotiate this rocky terrain today? Put another way, if it has become necessary to think about interfolded planetary temporalities that help to constitute a world containing moments of real creativity, what is the best way to pursue truth?

Remember, many people today experience themselves—particularly through exploratory engagements with others—as periodic participants in innovations in the domains of artistic production, food recipes, scientific theory, metaphysical speculation, political strategy, dietary habits, literary inventions, farming practices, or sociopolitical ideals. We resist the cohort of scientists—and many other scientists themselves resist such modes of reductionism too—who treat such experiences as appearances reducible in principle to deeper modes of determination. At least the theorists of complete determinism have not yet succeeded in proving such a wild metaphysical conjecture. It is a highly contestable faith or speculation, as Whitehead would say, one that also cuts against the intuitive experience of many. So we ask, how is it possible to support the intuition of periodic pulses of creativity—an intuition that helps to make life worth living—as you pursue truth? What, indeed, are the relations between presumptive care for the rich fecundity of the world, pulses of creative change that work upon solid stabilizations, and the lure of truth?

The task at issue is pursued by composing a dialogue between "F" and "W." F starts as Michel Foucault, a thinker who had a significant impact on my thinking in the 1980s and continues to influence me. W begins as Alfred North Whitehead, a thinker in the minor tradition who started to influence my thinking around 2005 or so and continues to do so. Foucault examined "disciplinary society" and several "regimes of truth" nestled in it. Periodically, previously legitimated or hidden suffering within a regime becomes more palpable through a combination of genealogical analysis and political protest.[14] A new regime may be forged in this or that domain. The interesting thing about a regime of truth is how it is composed of multiple interfolded elements: disciplines, methodological rules, assumptions, faiths, rhetorical strategies of inclusion and exclusion, testing devices, perceptual habits, and aspirations. The elements do not always move in tandem, however; so a regime can periodically become out of sorts with itself.

Whitehead supported a coherence model of truth set in the speculation that there are pulses of real creativity in a world also marked by zones of stability. He folded a theory of intersecting temporalities of heterogeneous sorts into the middle of his philosophy of science and processual view of the world, doing so to make sense of both modes of stabilization and periods of becoming that alter them.

His philosophy, because it extends elements of agency beyond the human estate, is even more radical in this respect than that of Foucault, though tremors of such ideas circulate through Foucault too. But in forging this path, Whitehead was much less alert than Foucault to various injuries done to prisoners, the mad, racial minorities, women, homosexuals, and boat people through the major disciplines and regimes of truth.

Whitehead, the brilliant logician, supplanted mind/body dualism, the subject/object binary, the life/nonlife dichotomy, substance foundationalism, the dichotomy between primary and secondary qualities, and deterministic images that prevailed in several European sciences and philosophies of his day. That is how he participated in the minor tradition. Most of these assumptions, assumed by many majoritarians to be embedded in logic itself, had helped to constitute the dominant regimes of truth in his day. Impressive. But it did not enter his mind to contest how, say, a regime of gender dualism was nested in the very debates between dominant European theologies, sciences, philosophies, court findings, corporate policies, and commonsense demands of his time—that is, how it was sustained by a multifaceted, major regime of truth.

What happens if you generate a dialogue between F and W that starts with positions each took during one phase of his thought and then allows each to refine some themes through both exchanges with the other and confrontation with new events that neither in fact encountered during his time?

As the dialogue continues, F and W become personae, intellectual figures of the past with continuing philosophical importance today. Their thinking thus begins to adjust through reciprocal exchanges and encounters with new events. The acceleration of planetary climate change is one such event, an event that both would have seized upon if it had come to sharp attention during their lives. But it did not, even though it was well underway. That latter event, indeed, would not only jostle both; it also speaks to the demeanor of self-modesty that each sought to fold into his own epistemological and ontological professions. Both posed surprises for their own generations and sensed that new surprises yet were apt to arrive. That is why Whitehead emphasized how important informed speculation is to philosophy, science, and social thought.

V

The agenda of the last essay, then, is one in which the correspondence model is transcended, pulses of real creativity are affirmed, coherence models are revised, explorations of subjective sensitivity are cultivated, attention to lures of a possible future are consulted, and festering remains from the past play roles in the pursuit of truth. An interplay between truth as regime and as lure is thereby projected. The element of periodic tension between a regime and a lure of truth is emphasized; the lure becomes dramatized most when the multiple elements that have composed a regime of truth begin to move out of synchronicity.

Such an approach scrambles the sense of necessity in a tired set of Euro-American logical binaries. In doing so, the door also opens to more reciprocal modes of exploratory communication with several non-Western traditions. For several of the latter traditions already resist human exceptionalism along with the binaries that have sustained it. Such an indispensable pursuit is not taken up extensively in this little study, though it does identify my recent attempts do so. More notably, it identifies reflective efforts by other recent thinkers in the minor tradition of Euro-American thought who have been forging such connections.

Truth now becomes simultaneously a thing of this world, a noble pursuit, problem oriented, subject to evolving methodological disciplines, and compatible with potential bouts of real creativity in the world. At any moment shocks and uncertainties may nudge some elements in a regime of truth, though the edges themselves tend to evolve over time. Whitehead came to such a view early in the twentieth century after he encountered the shock theories of relativity and quantum mechanics posed to the Newtonian theory he and others had so recently treated as apodictic. Newtonians had thought that only a few minor amendments were needed to consolidate a theory that corresponds to the world itself, when in fact, over a few explosive years, the whole regime imploded. Whitehead seems to think that you are better equipped to probe complex relations between time, historic subjectivities, speculation, and truth after you face a crisis in a theory you had thought to be apodictic. Truth now becomes a composite formation. He worries about dogmatism, in science, theology, philosophy, and the humanities, without turning to relativism. The latter stance is not pulled by a lure to truth that exceeds it.

The challenges this impressive logician and mathematician poses to a series of binary logics widely in circulation when he wrote are exemplary. Foucault, on the other hand, found himself painted into a corner as a gay man until he challenged several assumptions and disciplinary practices that had cornered him and many others in a variety of subject positions. He, too, resisted a set of hegemonic binaries authoritatively designed to inform inquiry in a neutral way.

We live during a time when similar things have been happening to neo-Darwinism, the geotheory of planetary gradualism, sharp versions of the life/nonlife dichotomy, theories of neoliberal capitalism, and the quaint idea that a separation of powers in democratic states will always suffice to ward off fascism. A hegemonic theory, even when it encounters several anomalies, can close out competitors for a time through its imposition of authoritative methods and arguments augmented by sharp ridicule of those ranging too far outside the fold. And then something happens that throws the assemblage into crisis. Now the lure of truth in a more open, fluid setting becomes particularly salient again.

Both Foucault and Whitehead exuded presumptive care for the actual and potential diversities of this world. That care must be presumptive because periodically forces seek to defeat and crush an ethos of diversity. Such forces must be opposed intelligently and militantly. The connection between a positive ethos of fecund life and the subtlety of inquiry—which may seem slender and unimportant to some at first—helps to fend off both the dreariness and dead ends of neopositivism and the reactive instigations to gleeful cruelty, big lies, and fake news defining the ethos of aspirational fascism. It does not suffice to do so, but it makes a difference. It is well to remember how some proponents of procedural democracy—conveying the sufficiency of separation of powers and checks and balances to a pluralist regime—underplayed the role that a positive ethos of sensitivity and presumptive generosity must play in giving life and direction to democratic institutions.

So, three interfolded essays. The first explores a few thinkers in the minor tradition who forged a path not pursued by enough others in Euro-American thought until late in the day. The second articulates the Anthropocene as a bumpy climate time machine composed of heterogeneous, intersecting temporalities. The third embraces the lure of truth, as it strives to devise workable balances between multiple elements in the face of new experiments and events.

One

Sophocles, Mary Shelley, and the Planetary

In a powerful chapter of *Shame and Necessity*, published in 1993, Bernard Williams confronts analytic philosophy—of which he was a noble practitioner—with themes advanced by Sophocles and Thucydides in fifth-century Greece.[1] Williams earlier in that book rejected readings that defined agency out of the philosophies and dramas of the Greeks or that acted as if Greek tragic fate had to mean a result preordained by the gods. And yet, once such exaggerated divisions between the Greeks and the moderns had been filtered out, another difference remained that distinguishes tragic thinkers from a powerful strain in Western thought embodied in the work of philosophers such as Plato, Aristotle, Augustine, Kant, and Hegel. It is not easy to state the shared assumption without folding exaggeration into the statement or misreading some thinkers on the list. These thinkers, too, disagreed radically among themselves. Plato thought (sometimes) that a few could gain mystical insight into the sphere of eternal ideas; Augustine thought that the unfathomable grace of God was needed to repair (even if not completely) divisions of the will that help to bring evil into a providential world; Kant thought that there was no reliable access to the world in itself but that, nonetheless, a series of transcendental arguments could show us how necessary it is to act as if we are free and as if an unbroken progress of cultural history is predisposed to us. And so it goes.

Amid those significant differences between the philosophers listed, Williams locates a set of affinities—affinities Nietzsche had earlier covered in two pages in *Twilight of the Idols* under the heading "How the Real World at Last Became a Myth."[2] What are they according to Williams? Well, the philosophers listed tended to think the nonhuman world of gods, or Ideas, or God, or history, nature, or substance is rather well disposed to our highest aims if we approach it through the right understandings, technologies, and/or spiritualities.

Sophocles (according to Williams) was resistant to such tendencies of thought: he focused on the effects of capricious gods upon the world in relation to volatile human passions. Thucydides, in turn, played up how chancy concatenations of nonhuman events and passions can periodically ignite consequences that could be disastrous for the protagonists.

Both thinkers contended, across the differences between them, that "there is nothing in the structure of the universe that denies the power (of human agents) to intend, to decide, to take or to receive responsibility."[3] That marks their points of affinity to each other. It is their emphasis on either the hostility of the gods or the concatenations of chancy events, however, that distinguishes Sophocles and Thucydides from many thinkers in the major tradition of European thought.[4]

At this juncture, it is best to allow Williams to speak for himself, as he seeks to project a perspective into analytic philosophy that emphasizes the play of contingency and unruly forces in the world. For Sophocles, there is "an order of things that has the shape and the discouraging effect of a hostile plan, a plan that remains incurably hidden from us." This contrasts with Hegel, for whom "there is a different illusion, hidden in the seductively phrased Hegelian claim that human beings are 'constituted' by society: the idea that the relations of human beings to society and to each other, if properly understood and properly enacted, can realize a harmonious identity that involves no real loss." Or so he could be amended to say, at least a final identity in which any losses are required by the highest achievements of being itself. The upshot, for Williams, is that tragic thinkers press the question, by comparison to major thinkers, "whether or not . . . beyond some things that human beings themselves have shaped there is anything at all that is intrinsically shaped to human interests, in particular to human ethical interests. In the light of that question ... Plato, Aristotle, Kant, Hegel are all on the same side."[5] Thucydides and Sophocles are on the other. He could have placed Heraclitus and Lucretius on the latter side too.

Though the references to oracles and gods in Greek tragic thought need to be naturalized, Williams thinks, the tragic traditions have much to say to modern life. We too should not suppose that, properly understood, the larger world is highly predisposed to us. Now, certainly, each of the major thinkers Williams identifies could find things to say in reply to his characterization of them. Kant, for instance, could point to the discrepancy between actual history and the point of view that must be postulated about historical progress if we are to act morally; Hegel could point to a series of hard necessities that must be accepted to foster the most harmonious modern world possible. And so on.

But such responses compare Williams's reading of Kant, Hegel, and so on to alternative readings of the same figures. It is surely important to determine which is the best reading of each. But Williams would contend, I think, that even if such issues of interpretation are resolved in favor of voices who dissent from his readings, a powerful set of differences persists between the major thinkers and the image of human relations to the larger world advanced by Greek tragedians. Those are the differences to ponder. Those are indeed the differences that Nietzsche preceded Williams in bringing to the fore, as Williams knows.

My judgments on this issue are closer to those of Williams and to the minor traditions he draws upon than to those of the major traditions he argues against. I say that, however, with three reservations. The first is that Williams did not pursue closely enough the ethical question of how to cultivate attachment to the larger world in the light of the rocky relationships he finds it to bear to human culture and history. We are intimately entangled with that larger world, and the Williams portrayal may underplay the intricacy of those entanglements. These are central concerns posed by Nietzsche and Michel Foucault, thinkers who otherwise disclose several points of contact with Williams.[6]

A second reservation takes the form of a question: What kind of shift in our styles of writing and presentation are needed if and when we come to terms with this issue in the way Williams recommends? While Zarathustra enacts responses to that very question, I will mostly leave it dangling here, though attention to the styles of Sophocles and Mary Shelley by comparison to that of Williams (and me) are surely pertinent.

The third item also takes the form of a question: Why is Williams so abstract in articulating the temporal volatilities of the world as they intersect with the historical adventures of human cultures? Neither Thucydides nor Sophocles was. Neither is a set of earth scientists who have recently shattered the assumptions of planetary gradualism that set the agenda for nineteenth- and twentieth-century earth scientists and filtered into the background assumptions of so many European cultural theorists.

To help relieve the abstract character of the Williams assertion, I turn first to Sophocles, then to Mary Shelley, and finally to contemporary earth science critiques of the story of planetary gradualism. The claims Williams advances may acquire more vitality and pertinence if the abstract containers in which he placed them are filled with dynamic relations between planetary forces and the vicissitudes of cultural life.

Oedipus at Colonus

The old, bedraggled man is led by his daughter toward a noble stand of trees just outside the city. He is blind and famous throughout Greece for the unspeakable horrors of killing his father, marrying his mother, replacing his father as king of Thebes, and siring four children through incest. It turns out that the two are now on the edge of a sacred grove outside Athens called Colonus, a place he is seeking as he and his daughter/sister wander from Thebes. The blind man has become a bit of an irascible visionary by now, perhaps similar to the now old Sophocles who called the Colonus deme his home. Trying to ward off wary citizens who seek to rid this sacred place of a vagabond, he tells them that it was foretold that he must end his life here. Apollo intimated that certain "signs would warn [him] of these things: earthquakes, thunder, lightnings from Zeus."[7]

We will not tarry over how the grove at Colonus recalls Prometheus, who was punished so severely by Zeus for giving fire to humans, or how Sophocles also invokes Poseidon, the god of raging seas, floods, droughts, and earthquakes, or how a straggle of Athenians there condemn Oedipus for his previous deeds, or how he explains repeatedly that the "deeds of horror" were the unintentional upshot of innocent actions he had taken within a divine order of gods hostile to his family line, or how Creon arrives from Thebes seeking to capture the two daughters and return the polluted girls to Thebes, or how Theseus, the sovereign of Athens, saves them, or how his daughter, Antigone—foreshadowing her later flouting in *Antigone* of this very maxim—warns everyone against the bad effects of "antagonistic acts."[8] We ask, rather, what makes the wise Theseus come to admire this blind, polluted wanderer and what lessons the story of Colonus may carry for life during the Anthropocene.

Consider, then, additional references to the volatility of the nonhuman world that punctuate this drama. There is the loud "clap of thunder" when the Chorus reviews dramatic shifts in fate and asks whether those shifts are foreordained or full of contingency. There is another loud peal that Oedipus interprets as a call to accept the call of Hades. There is soon a "crack that shatters the air, followed by lightning." And soon the Chorus chants:

> Louder, louder, hear it?—crashing down
> Divine report, dumbstriking sound
> Picking up my hair with panic and shattering my soul
> there, again! Light rips the sky
> I'm stricken to the core with fear.
> Such a pregnant rush of light
> Never comes without meaning
> Never not with monstrous issue—
> Great, awful sky! Zeus, oh save us.[9]

Later, after Oedipus once again faces "these fulminating bolts of unanswerable artillery," Theseus prepares to bury the old vagabond with honor in the sacred grove itself.[10] As Oedipus disappears from sight, buried in a grave site never to be found, "there came a grumbling sound from Zeus's underworld."[11] Another earth tremor. Finally, Theseus reports to the loyal daughters/sisters of Oedipus that during the very hour of his death "no white hot thunderbolt from Zeus came down."[12]

Don't make the humanist mistake of interpreting these planetary interruptions as merely symbols of things going on within the life of an individual or culture. They are that, but to grasp them as symbolic in such a sense alone is to place yourself too close to the major tradition that Sophocles and Williams each challenges in his own way. For it is dangerous, both say, to treat nonhuman planetary processes as regular and gradual unless and until radical human intervention into them occurs.[13] One way to put it is to say that the timing of these events is symbolic to some (though not all) of the characters in the plays of Sophocles while the volatile processes themselves are also etched into the very fabric of Greek life. Greece itself sits close to a dynamic tectonic conjuncture in the Mediterranean where the Northern Aegean plate presses south, an African plate presses north, and a smaller Eurasian plate presses east. The three plates are also marked by differences in rock density and weight. The result is a volatile zone punctuated by numerous earthquakes, volcanoes, and tsunamis of differing strengths.[14] It is a turbulent place.

The experience of tragic possibility in Greek life is closely bound to an awareness of volatile, nonhuman processes, whether interpreted through the lens of gods or (as by some) naturalistically. Plagues populate the stories, playing key roles in them. Zeus both personifies thunder and lightning and expresses Greek awareness of nonhuman forces that periodically lurch out of sync with themselves—or at least break from the steadiness and regularity humanists often seek to find in them. A lightning bolt strikes when the atmosphere has become unbalanced; it follows a jagged path made possible by that imbalance. A tremor, volcano, earthquake, or tsunami explodes suddenly after two tectonic plates have rubbed slowly against each other.

The wise Sophocles does not treat such events only as symbols, then. He also sees them as real, turbulent forces, whether filled with divine animation, as most characters in his plays profess, or both fraught and devoid of divinity, as a few characters in his plays assert and several intellectuals of that day contended.

The fact that many citizens filled such events with divine intentions and drives was countered by contemporary intellectuals who both denied the role of divinity in them and emphasized planetary turbulence more than many modern thinkers do. It is not clear that Williams, for instance, marks these tremors in the dramas of Sophocles.

Jocasta, in *Oedipus the King*, flirted with the view that the gods were intrinsically unimportant to Greek life before she took her own life. Is it certain that she recanted that view just before committing suicide in the face of the incredible shame she would feel once the bad news spread about her marriage and children? The Messenger in *Antigone* may have held nonthe-istic views, himself, as he both affirmed the theme of a wayward world and doubted that there was a "reliable horoscope for man" through which to read it.

Indeed, Hesiod's *Theogony*, composed a few centuries before *Oedipus at Colonus*, in which the final fight between the Olympians and Titans takes the shape of a cosmic fireworks display replete with massive earthquakes, volcanic eruptions, lightning, and unbearable storms, may hearken to a time several hundred years before the oral tradition was written, when the most advanced island city-state of the day—then called Thera and now Santorini—was destroyed by a huge volcanic eruption, one of the largest on the skin of the earth for the last ten thousand years. The plume shot up two miles, and a tsunami flooded Crete; it may possibly have provided (though this is intensely debated) the experiential basis for the Red Sea crossing in the story of Exodus.[15] That holocaust probably set back Greek culture a few hundred years.[16] Sophocles would certainly have been aware of the massive quake that rattled Sparta in 464 BCE and sparked a helot rebellion.

Such recurrent events in Hesiod and Sophocles are thus both symbols of disturbances in the life of the culture and historical expressions of the volatile nature of the nonhuman world within which Greek life was (and is) set. The forces themselves affect profoundly the contours and chal-lenges of cultural life.

An exclusively symbolic reading of such forces was one tendency in twentieth-century thought that may have helped to set back the humani-ties and human sciences in Europe and the United States, slowing down the pace at which they came to terms with the regime of the Anthropo-cene and, especially, the recurrent imbrications between cultural triggers, cosmic forcings, and planetary amplifiers in the production and accelera-tion of what is now called the Anthropocene. It also may have been one reason that many moderns have often been inclined to interpret Greek tragic ideas of fate through the lens of Greek notions of divine preordain-ment rather than focusing as well on counterthemes in Greek life itself that tie fate to hubristic actions conjoined to an unfortunate concatena-tion of human and nonhuman contingencies. To hitch the latter reading to Greek images of volatile nonhuman processes is to draw a tragic image of possibility closer to the vicissitudes of late modern life.

Theseus honors the blind old vagabond in part because the horrific adventure of the visionary makes him an emblem of how the nonhuman world—divine or natural, as the case may be—is volatile and not reliably predisposed to human welfare, how, joined to that, terrible things sometimes happen despite the good intentions of the agents involved. Indeed, if good intentions express naive background assumptions about either the benign character of the gods when you are pious or the strong predisposition of gradual planetary processes to either human mastery or harmony with them, things are more often apt to go wrong. This is a lesson Bernard Williams drew from the tragedies of Sophocles, though he did not carry that lesson into the heart of the Anthropocene.

Hell is paved with the good intentions of naive believers and nonbelievers; such intentions sometimes place inordinate demands upon a planet treated primarily as a theater of human action. The naive, brilliant Oedipus had noble intentions in that first drama when he solved the riddle posed by the Sphinx.

It is not only the Greek tragic traditions that evince awareness of such nonhuman forces; some minor elements within Jewish traditions have done so too.[17] Indeed, a conversation could be launched between orientations to spiritual awakenings across these creedal traditions. Certainly, the theophany in the *Book of Job* would support such exchanges, as the Nameless One eventually recites a litany of volatile forces and powerful animals to Job that both exceed the capacities of humanity to tame and may suggest that the world was not created to give priority to humans alone. And, as already noted, some contested readings of Exodus have traced the lineages of the Red Sea crossing back to the earthy shock of the Thera quake. Perhaps some Christian ideas about a limited God fit such a rocky frame too, as Catherine Keller suggests in a reading of Genesis that presents a biblical Creator who found a bubbling Deep already there as he began to design the world.[18] The Deep provided the fecund, volatile materials that enabled and limited creation of the world.

Such conjunctions between diverse spiritual traditions, care for the world, and appreciation of planetary volatility could add fuel to social movements today drawn from a plurality of final sources to press diverse regions, states, temples, universities, labor movements, and corporations to acknowledge the volatility of planetary forces, to admit, as Pope Francis has, the differential contributions some religious traditions have made to the current agonies of the Anthropocene, to articulate its differential effects on diverse regions and constituencies, and to take rapid action in each domain to reverse the current trajectory of things.[19] Given the urgency of time, consolidation of a militant assemblage already in the works and drawn from diverse sources and places to mobilize cross-regional actions is needed today. They could even converge in cross-regional general strikes. The potential power of such strikes is that they would work on the relevant institutions from inside and outside simultaneously.[20]

It may be—to channel Cornel West—that some bearers of prophetic Christianity who confess the advent of Jesus as a loving force in a world of spiritual diversities are more amenable to such tectonic shifts in thinking, judgment, and action than many bearers of Constantinian Christianity, though some of the latter, emphasizing the contestability of their own faith, have moved in this direction.[21] The task is to incite relations of agonistic respect between carriers of different theo-cosmologies who then assemble to support a militant cross-regional assemblage to respond to the regionally distributed assaults of galloping climate change. Such interruptions of political life as usual must involve, among several other things, the active pursuit of spiritual affinities across creedal differences between the activists.

The Year without a Summer

In April 1815, Mount Tambora on the isle of Sumbawa in Indonesia exploded. The ensuing explosions, among the most intense in the last several thousand years, continued for days. Sulfur plumes shot up into the stratosphere; over seventy thousand people died; the monsoon over India was soon interrupted; average global temperatures declined by around 1.3 degrees Fahrenheit over the next three years; several areas of the world experienced crop failures or declines; and cholera soon spread through several regions of the world.[22]

The spread of cholera was correlated with the dispersion of the plume and its climatic effects. How? Well, the best guess seems to be that an increase in plankton in stagnant waterways fed the cholera bacteria, as the bacteria also mutated under these favorable conditions to become more flexible, potent, and adaptive. "In 1817 the aquatic environment of the Bay of Bengal had deteriorated radically owing to the disrupted monsoon, a consequence of Tambora's dimming presence in the stratosphere. By a process that remains mysterious in its details the altered estuarine ecology then stimulated an unprecedented event of genetic mutation in the ancient career of the cholera bacterium."[23]

Regional droughts induced by the volcanic eruption and the increased rainfall it spawned in other regions unfortunately contributed to the same result: the loss of the monsoon increased the temperature of standing bodies of water in some regions, and the excessive rain elsewhere (as in Europe) also encouraged the growth of nutrients for the virulent bacteria.[24]

Volcanic eruptions have played an important role in the bumpy history of this planet. It is probable that snowball earth itself was first disrupted by a massive set of volcanic eruptions. Such eruptions cool things for a while and later warm the planet as the CO_2 emissions secreted linger in the atmosphere to warm the planet long after the larger dust particles blocking the sun have settled to earth. The sulfur emissions propelled high into the stratosphere by the Tambora eruption combined with sun dimming already operative in the late stages of the Little Ice Age to cool temperatures, create massive food shortages, and increase rain volume in Europe. The sun dimming already in force was due to the cyclical decline in sunspot activity. In some places, such as Germany, the unfortunate timing of these two events together created severe food shortages and sparked riots.

Mary Shelley, Lord Byron, and Percy Shelley lived in Switzerland during the summer of 1816, often gathering at Byron's estate in Geneva. Various romances and sexual adventures ensued, sparked in part by Mary's half-sister Claire, who had affairs with both Byron and Mary's husband Percy, and further prodded by the apparently omnisexual appetite of Byron. Percy Shelley had earlier proposed a ménage à trois between him, his first wife, and Mary, but the proposal fell apart. As Percy Shelley said in one letter to a countess about the summer of 1816: "The natives of Geneva . . . did not hesitate to affirm that we were leading a life of unbridled libertinism. . . . I will only tell you that atheism, incest, and many other things—sometimes ridiculous and sometimes terrible—were imputed to us."[25] The cold days and nights seemed to incite exploratory passions among the small band of experimentalists: wild acts bristling with yet other possibilities not taken.

The expected summer weather did not arrive until late during their stay in Geneva. Instead they faced rainy, very cold days, with cloudy, colder nights. One dismal night Byron proposed that each of them compose a ghost or horror story to entertain the others. Mary started hers; eventually it emerged full blown as *Frankenstein: Prometheus Unbound*.

The story, rich, evocative, and chilling, has received diverse modes of appreciation. Did Mary paint an allegory of the subordinate place of women? Yes, her mother, who died shortly after her birth, was Mary Wollstonecraft, and her father, the radical William Godwin, supported new rights for women though he was severe from time to time with the girls and women in his household. Does the story offer a critique of the rise of aggressive scientific attempts to master nature? Certainly. Is Victor Frankenstein, the novel's creator of the monster who remains unnamed in the long text, beset by oedipal relations with his father and the cousin he was scheduled to marry? Yes, these too find expression in projections of the tale. Was the ever-elusive creature itself a double of Victor Frankenstein, produced by its creator to carry out murders Victor unconsciously desired but could not condone? Very probably. Did the story open a door to readings of it as an allegory of racial hierarchy? Yes. Did Mary Shelley, the author, struggle with ambivalence toward her dashing, freewheeling, heroic mate, who both lavished praise upon her and engaged in sexual and poetic experiments that tested those attachments? Again, these too seem to find expression in the text. What about Victor, the scientist who collects parts from dead beings like refuse in order to assemble a new being out of them? Does the subtitle, *Prometheus Unbound*, point allegorically to new consolidations of capital as it devours humans and nature for its use and leaves piles of rubble behind? I concur with others in saying so.

The story line suggests several such entanglements, as creator and creature find themselves at different moments replicating the shifting moods, traits, and actions of the other. The drive to implacable revenge, to take a pivotal example, migrates from Victor's creature to Victor's own quest to destroy it and back again to the creature, growing with intensity at each crossing. The story also poses issues of timing and location that cast the sufficiency of several such interpretations into doubt. It may even stymie any self-contained cultural story, even one couched in the psychoanalytic categories projected back upon it today.

Touched by the above issues, I nonetheless focus on three related dimensions of the story. All of them are bound to the fact that Mary Shelley experienced summer that year, not as a regular turn in a regular cycle of seasons, but as a fragile formation that could collapse suddenly. The first reading speaks to tremors of potentiality simmering in the consolidations of Shelley's prose in ways that may bring out the fungibility and fragility of the things she does experience. The second notes the appearance of this story during a time when images of evolution of humans from other forms of life once again excited the imagination of adventurers and poets—Mary and Percy Shelley among them. The third speaks to the sudden shifts in weather and terrain that punctuate the story.

The unnamed creature, slave, monster, wretch, demon, fiend, or devil, as he was called by Victor at different moments, was a huge physical specimen. Upon his escape from Eden shortly after creation, he performed incredible feats of strength, displayed superhuman speed, and enacted complex schemes that might put even Byron to shame. He was a precursor to Superman, minus the latter's role as a savior to citizens who bestow dangerous authority and trust upon him.

The creature at first displayed an innocent set of warm affections, sympathies, and skills, some of them perhaps generated from remains and traces of thought-imbued passion left behind in the dead adult brain implanted into its head and given life in its body. Since it was cloned from adult body parts, its initial actions are neither the result simply of genetic traits nor of a purity of being entirely uncontaminated by prior experience. Mary thus salutes the layered character of memory in noncloned humans, too, in which the earliest experiences are not recollected later; rather, they find expression in embedded dispositions to feeling, judgment, and action—memory, not only as recollection but also as layered into dispositions, tendencies, and premonitions that pop up in specific situations.

The creature learned quickly. He soon found—despite the escapee's attempts to provide secret aid to the poor family in the cabin he had selected for prolonged bouts of voyeurism in order to learn language, modes of social intercourse, and skills—that his monstrous appearance frightened and repulsed the household and all other humans. His irregular gait, huge proportions, ugly head, translucent skin, vacant eyes, and strange facial expressions were too much for them to endure.

Here is his self-characterization, after he had escaped the house of the creator and acquired sufficient self-consciousness:

Of my creation and creator I was absolutely ignorant. But I knew that I possessed no money, no friends, no kind of property. I was, besides, endowed with a figure hideously deformed and loathsome; I was not even of the same nature as man. I was more agile than they, and could subsist upon a coarse diet; I bore the extremes of heat and cold with less injury to my frame; my stature exceeded theirs. When I looked around, I saw and heard none like me. Was I then a monster, a blot upon the earth, from which all men fled and whom all men disowned?[26]

He morphed rapidly from a caring wretch overflowing with sympathy for others and yearning to belong to a larger community into a raging being who sought revenge against those who repudiated him and the monster who had created him. He became remarkably similar to those "armored males" Klaus Theweleit studied who formed the initial battering rams of the Nazi movement in Germany.[27] Recollections of *Prometheus Bound* and premonitions of *Blade Runner* also circulate through this compelling tale. Prometheus disobeyed Zeus to give fire to needy humans and suffered immense pain for doing so. The monster escaped another Zeus to anonymously bestow firewood upon the sweet, poor family living under his secret gaze. The care and daring of both figures invited the wrath of the gods who sought to rule them.

Keeping in mind the rocky, uncertain connections between the anonymous dispositions folded into him and the new experiences he encountered, consider a few junctures in the story replete with nanomoments of possibility peeking through the consolidations. Shelley is alert to moments of action in which what might or could have become enters into the mutability of the "is." She plays with received nature/culture distinctions in several ways.

We speak, then, of "ifs" poised on the edges of experience and relations, as a flirtation does, or a temptation, or a stutter, or a suppressed premonition, showing how action and practice often bristle with untaken potentialities poised on their edges.

What if, say, the monster had impregnated Elizabeth on the day of her wedding with Victor instead of killing her? A big if, certainly, residing in the fraught uncertainty of the reader's initial encounter with the scene. Victor hears a scream and races to find Elizabeth draped across the bridal bed in a white wedding gown with her head hanging just over the bed's edge. Does the scene, so carefully described, intimate for a nanosecond that she had just been ravished by one alpha male to take revenge against another alpha male? One monster with an engorged penis using a woman to take revenge against that other monster—Victor—with an engorged head? The question mark at the inception of the scene continues to hover over it even after we find that Elizabeth was killed, making you wonder again whether the creature is a double of Victor—as Iago, whose whispers were so insistent, functioned as a double of Othello.

Such a rape scene, if consolidated in the prose, would outrage the public of the day and could well stop the book from being published. But the choreography of the scene does hint at such a possibility, before it dissolves into the death of Elizabeth—the cousin Victor loved so dearly and toward whom he felt such ambivalence.

Such an if, poised on the verge of action, might have allowed the wretch to propagate future generations that help to turn the human evolutionary line more rapidly in a new direction. Such a result would perhaps be close to the very recent knowledge of how Neanderthals and Homo sapiens did mate, even though most evolutionary biologists committed to a treelike model of evolution had denied that very possibility until DNA results supported it.

A host of ifs circulate through the actualities of the *Frankenstein* tale, then, some intimated by the author and others by readers of the fraught story in new settings. For instance, did Victor, the first one to find his bride dead on the bridal bed, kill her himself during a lost moment when he had sunk into the dark world of that elusive double?

These are dark ifs. But if all ifs—pluripotentialities residing in incipient processes on the way to reduction into specific acts—were drained from the texture of experience and action, things would become gray and drab, sunk into a fog of dreary days. The edges of experience would lose the incitements to imagination from which poetry, flirtations, novels, philosophies, humor, adventures, creative strategies, premonitions, and new scientific experiments are born.

I retain the sense of untaken possibilities hovering in life as we turn to our second issue: the cloudy image of species evolution that inhabits this tale. Mary and Percy Shelley were well aware of the work of Erasmus Darwin (1731–1802), the grandfather of Charles Darwin. Erasmus had himself advanced a preliminary image of biological evolution at odds with the dominant Christian temper that charged the culture of the day. Evolution presented itself to him as a possible alternative to divine creation from nothing. The elder Darwin did not seem to embrace the interventionist, hubristic image of science that inflamed Victor Frankenstein after he studied chemistry. At least Victor imbibed such an aggressive image until recanting it much later, after witnessing the fruits of that production.

Erasmus was impressed with what today would be called the self-organizing processes in species evolution. In such an image, the strivings of multiple intersecting entities, such as mutations, bacteria, and embryos, periodically enter into resonances with one another. Occasionally a new species emerges out of those that is irreducible to the simple replication of mutations alone.[28] Evolution as self-organizing processes often enough includes horizontal processes exceeding the vertical processes involved in sexual relations.

Such an image of species evolution encourages less hubristic practices of science than those advanced today by proponents of climate geoengineering, cloning, nuclear physics, behavioral social science, neo-Darwinism, and—most generically—the pursuit of human mastery over a docile earth. It rather encourages scientists to watch and study life forms to gauge the multiple strivings, resonances, horizontal intersections, and bifurcation points through which evolution proceeds. A bifurcation point issues at least one if and one course actually taken. Sophocles would call it a crossroad.

Here is one quotation from Erasmus Darwin in 1794 that suggests the direction of his poetic imagination of evolution. Perhaps, he says, "in the great depth of time, since the earth began to exist, it would not be too bold to imagine, that all warm blooded animals were arisen from one living filament . . . possessing the faculty of continuing to improve by its own inherent artistry, and of delivering those improvements by generation to posterity."[29] The filament of life becomes transfigured into the spark of life by Victor. Knowing the power of electricity, he applies huge jolts of it to the assemblage of limbs, organs, and body parts he has collected from human cadavers and animals, doing so to impart life to a dead mass of materials assembled together.

The first statement by Erasmus, however, must be balanced against others in which he contends that, while there is progress within a cosmic epoch, over vast stretches of time each epoch dissolves only to arise again out of chaos to repeat itself. "Thus all the suns, and the planets, which circle around them, may again sink into central chaos; and may again by explosions produce a new world: which in the process of time may resemble the present one and at length again undergo the same catastrophe."[30]

We can discern another twist in the Erasmus image of evolution through the recent work of Terrence Deacon. His major quest, too, is to study how life could have emerged from nonlife. He does so by hypothesizing how self-organized, complex molecules of different sorts resonated together after chance contact until life emerged. Each complex possessed some traits needed for life; neither could generate it out of its own resources alone. Deacon also contends that, absent the liveliness of a quantum world, life may well have not emerged out of such a spontaneous intersection. He asserts, however, that quantum liveliness does not become life until two diverse sets of complex molecules meet, with each possessing some of the qualities needed for the advent of life. Here we hear an echo from Erasmus minus the assumption of necessary evolutionary progress within a cosmic epoch.

Deacon detects a processual self-organization of life, with the word "self" conveying, not a centralized agency, but modes of spontaneous intersection between trajectories without outside control. Neither God nor Victor is needed. Because self-organization is replete with pluripotentialities on the way, humans who seek to adopt the God role themselves may create a monster. Here are a few quotations from Deacon's text:

> The scientific problem is that there aren't ultimate particles or simple "atoms" devoid of lower level compositional organization on which to ground unambiguous higher level distinctions of causal power. Quantum theory has dissolved this base at the bottom. . . . Quantum fields have ambiguous spatiotemporal origins with extended properties that are only statistical and dynamically definitive, defined by a wave function.
>
> . . . It is necessary to understand how the material and energetic threads of the universe became entangled in just the right way as to produce an additional dimension that is the fabric of both life and mind.
>
> Although the transition from a non-teleological dynamic to a teleodynamically organized molecular system constituted a fundamental transition in the cosmic history of causality . . . it necessarily involved a simple combination of molecular processes.[31]

Deacon is closer to Erasmus Darwin than to either Victor's drive to clone a servant or neo-Darwinian views of genetic determination. The latter theorists, indeed, are unable to provide a plausible interpretation of how nonlife could have transitioned into life because the prelife nature they portray is so dead and mechanical. For Deacon, again, the process of transfiguration involved two sets of complex molecules interacting after being placed in a chancy conjunction.

Deacon is probably unlike Erasmus Darwin in one respect: the fecund materials from which life is said to emerge and then to evolve carry no guarantee with them that evolution will regularly work to the advantage of humans. His theory of evolution would become even more rich (and bumpy) by joining the protean bio-theme of teleodynamism to new geological understandings that at key junctures planetary convulsions have both decimated old species and set in motion new possibilities for teleodynamic coalescence.

What about Mary Shelley? Her story seems to appreciate the self-organizing capacities of nonhuman processes, as it worries immensely about wayward forces set into motion by a hubristic human creator who does not respect the multiple ways creations can morph through new experiences beyond the anticipations of the creator. Does Mary project automatic progress into evolution if and when it is left to its own devices? We do not get a clear answer to that question in the text, but there are hints and premonitions that open a door to exploration of the idea that there is no assured connection between the autonomous turns of evolution and its progress in a way that is favorable to humanity. Some of those hints are located in the discussions of climate and terrain to be explored soon.

Shelley disturbs received nature/culture distinctions. Consider the horror people feel when they first confront the monster. Is that feeling both inborn and fixed? Well, perhaps, but consider the undercurrent of fascination that rumbles through the horror. This fascination could eventually propel you to explore how nonhuman beings are invested with strivings and capacities of interconnection that exceed the demands of those invested with the remains of Cartesianism. Victor, after all, was fascinated as a young man by Paracelsus before it was knocked out of him by his chemistry teacher. Paracelsus was the thinker who located multiple strivings and purposes in plants and animals touched in different ways by the hand of God.

An octopus is as monstrous to Cartesians, at first encounter, as was this monster to those who encountered it. Its appearance is strange. Cartesians would deny purpose, striving, and thought to the octopus. Upon closer study, however, distinctive modes of organization and coordination are discernible between separate regions of experience in the octopus. Its complex improvisations in water, coral reefs, food quests, and predator avoidance stymie analogies between it and human modes of being; they also disclose it to possess complex intentions, skills, and strivings as a being. We are landlubbers whose evolution took different trails from that of the octopus; it long preceded us and continues to evolve alongside us. We no longer need to see it as a monster; we might even, upon close attention to its wondrous mode of being, stop destroying the coral settings in which it thrives.

Does Mary Shelley imagine that evolution has intrinsic ups and downs—nay, that it follows wayward paths with no universal standard of measure through which to assess every actual and possible path as progressive or regressive? What species, anyway, is qualified to measure the long, bumpy course of evolution? Is the agent of measurement to select itself as the standard, concentrating its assessment of temporal progress or regress upon the traits through which it excels? What about the suspicion that if a common measure could be found, blue whales—with their complex powers of long-range communication and ability to close down one side of the brain to sleep while the other side stays awake—would prove superior to humans? We are not good at closing down one half of the brain while keeping the other side awake while cruising the ocean. How much is proved by the fact that we are better equipped to kill whales than they are to kill us? The monster fared well on that last criterion.

We dwell, then, on premonitions hovering on the edges of Mary's thought about evolution, the sort of premonitions that enabled her to conceive this tale itself out of the dissonant conjunctions between a harsh stepmother, a famous radical father, an intense and wide education, a smart, wayward husband, a cold summer, her brilliance as a writer, and ambivalences incited by a turbulent time with that volatile crew in Geneva—the sort of premonitions that could well have opened her to new evidence about the history of planetary volatility if such evidence had become available during that strange year without a summer.

Could Mary Shelley even suspect that this reemerging faith in species evolution set on a progressive plane still expressed an unconscious hangover from an old theology of an omnipotent, creative God who presides over human progress, a theology that Erasmus had tried to overturn? That is, does Victor's hubris, to her, create the only rent in an otherwise beneficent, progressive evolution? I don't know. But it was unexpectedly cold that summer, in a way that challenged the steady expectation of seasonal change. Without attributing such a view to Mary herself, loose threads in the story can be pulled to suggest that evolution is a bumpy process entangled with multiple forces and agencies of numerous sorts that do not assume a treelike shape of progress. The scene in which Victor finally tears apart the new wife-in-the-making he had promised (in a weak moment) as a mate to the lonely wretch—just before the new creation was completed— may suggest such an idea without demanding it.

Mary does seem drawn to an image of self-organization in nature expressed through the rich poetic speculations of Erasmus Darwin; she also invites wariness about the hubris of masterful scientists who seek to use, shape, and dominate nature for the material advancement of people living under the cover of capitalism, empire, and human mastery. The support Erasmus Darwin gave to women's rights and the end of slavery fits the worldview I draw from him and her without insisting that these are necessarily their views.

We have wandered a bit, thinking, first, about ifs not taken hovering on the edges of the actions and relations of this tale and, second, about its premonitions about species evolution before the time of Charles Darwin. A third feature of the tale is, however, most significant for the purposes of our reflection; it also helps to entangle the first two together. You could draw upon it to complicate the discussion of evolution already launched.

The assembled lovers and adventurers at the Byron estate found themselves stuck together during evenings because, again, 1816 was the year without a summer. They did not know the Tambora volcano had generated this condition by triggering a series of amplifiers such as lingering dust in the stratosphere to block sun rays, a drop in temperatures, more extensive rains in Europe, the loss of crops in parts of Asia and Europe, local famines, an upsurge of cholera, the weakening of monsoons in Asia, and the conjunction of these events with a Little Ice Age that was already in its late stages. But they were alert to the unruly weather formations that summer. And Erasmus himself had speculated about the possible role of volcanic eruptions in the origin of life.

Victor, his creature, his father, his best friend, his younger brother, Justine (the poor cousin falsely executed for killing the younger brother), and his bride-to-be encounter multiple forces, agencies, passions, and events that work back and forth upon each other. Sublime and volatile forces inform the world of *Frankenstein* because Mary Shelley was alert—like Sophocles before her—to how multiple nonhuman forces and agencies can infuse, disrupt, inspire, and pummel human life. As the narrator announces somewhere in this story, "The only thing constant in this world is mutability."

Consider a few examples of such strange, unruly mutabilities, as they arouse passions, turn events, or dissolve prior intentions:

- Victor, in a vicious storm after the death of his young brother, William: the "vivid flashes of lightning dazzled my eyes, illuminating the lake, making it appear like a vast sheet of fire. . . . The storm . . . appeared at once in various parts of the heavens . . . this noble war in the sky elevated my spirits."

- On a desperate trek into the Alps with Elizabeth to find and kill the monster: "As we ascended still higher, the valley assumed a magnificent and astonishing character . . . ; we heard the rumbling of the falling avalanche, and marked the smoke of its passage."

- Traversing the Mont Blanc glacier: "Presently a breeze dissipated the cloud, and I descended upon the glacier. The surface is very uneven, rising like the waves of a troubled sea . . . ; the field of ice is almost a league in width and I spent nearly two hours in crossing it."

- As the chase of the speedy, elusive "demon" accelerates, pulling Victor across "immense deserts" to the frozen sea: "I continued with unabated fervor to traverse immense deserts, until the ocean appeared at a distance. . . . Oh!, how unlike it was to the blue seas of the south! Covered with ice it was only to be distinguished from land by its superior wildness and ruggedness."

- Finally, while closing in on his elusive prey as he crosses a jagged, frozen section of ocean on a sledge: "A ground sea was heard; the thunder of its progress, as the waters rolled and swelled beneath me, became every moment more ominous and terrific. . . . The wind arose; the sea roared and, with the mighty shock of an earthquake, it split and cracked with a tremendous, and overwhelming sound. The work was soon finished: within a few minutes a tumultuous sea rolled between me and my enemy, and I was left drifting on a scattered piece of ice."[32]

This is a mere sampling of wild encounters in *Frankenstein* with turbulent rivers, expansive oceans, overhanging ledges, sharp, piercing sounds, diseases, Alpine glaciers, immense deserts, torrential rains, Arctic ice regions, bacterial invasions, and shattering ice packs. The multiple shifts in the mood of Victor—with courage, despair, hubris, new energy, sympathy, and vengeance notable among the ones that cycle in and out. The moods are not merely symbolized by these encounters in the way an upsurge of music in an old film signals rising passions the viewers are not allowed to see reach fruition because of restrictive film codes. No, such encounters slide, slip, or burst into the sensorium, engendering vague, intense precursors to the moods and purposes that do emerge. The moods are not determined by the precursors; the precursors serve as incipiencies or prompts that are then sharpened or modified through conscious thought. The creature, suspended uncertainly between humanity and monstrosity, feels such precursors and vague premonitions in ways that may help us to better appreciate the role they play in our everyday lives. Mutability is a recurrent feature of this world.

We must valorize, above all, those rapid breaks and transitions between extremes of heat and cold, level ground and rocky terrain, desert and ocean, ice flows and river currents, highlands and lowlands that punctuate the story. They show how alert Mary Shelley was to extremities of weather, climate, and terrain during a short period on a relatively small slice of territory ranging between Switzerland, France, England, Scotland, and the outskirts of the Artic. It would not take much more—if the new earth sciences had arrived in time—to convince the poetic author that deep, sometimes rapid temporal shifts occur in the ocean conveyor system, glacier fields, climate processes, ocean levels, degrees of ocean acidification, drought zones, monsoon configurations, storm patterns, atmospheric carbon and oxygen levels, and turns in species evolution. The spatial adventure with temporal undertones Mary Shelley imagined could now be stretched into longer temporal adventures replete with several bumpy tipping points.

Mary and Percy had visited Mount Vesuvius and read about its previous eruptions. Their challenges to Christian providentialism, through the lens of Charles Percy's vitalist-atheism, provided one prompt for a new perspective during a time when the terms of the dominant Christian faith in an omnipotent God discouraged and punished such exploratory ventures.[33] The Vesuvius visit and the strange summer of 1816 opened other doors. Indeed, Mary's story, if given a temporal tilt, could be transfigured into a geocultural history of strategic intersections between species evolution and rocky planetary processes. Planetary history itself would now become long, bumpy, and spatiotemporal, a veritable historicization of planetary processes that works to reconfigure the contours of those more familiar cultural histories.

To put it more generically, if the image of species evolution involving diverse modes of self-organization that Erasmus Darwin and Terrence Deacon advance in different ways were conjoined to the periodic advent of massive volcanic eruptions, asteroid hits, and shifts in ocean currents, glacier flows, drought zones, and climate patterns, the nineteenth-century picture of an evolutionary tree advanced by Charles Darwin would morph into a series of tangled bushes branching out in diverse directions. So let's transfigure the Shelley image of planetary extremities into a story of intersecting planetary temporalities with periodic junctures of volatility between them. Inspired in part by Sophocles and Shelley, we launch such a transfiguration in the next section, to be consolidated in the second essay.

Sociocentrism and Planetary Temporalities

Sociocentrism, in its most naive modern guise, is the tacit idea that social processes can be explained sufficiently by reference to other social processes alone. According to this image, planetary conditions lurk in the background of social life as slow-moving environments, settings, landscapes, or geographical contexts. Sure, you must fend off industrial pollution of waterways and the atmosphere, but the sources of those problems come from human cultures alone.

European sociocentrists disagree radically among themselves, of course, about which social factors exert the most influence upon others. Some contend that self-balancing processes within a privately incorporated market economy promise endless growth, while others locate internal contradictions within capital that generate class exploitation, ruthless colonization, periodic crisis, and social unrest. Very different views: if those were the only options, I would support the second over the first.

But these parties do tend to complement one another in another way: each tends to concentrate intensely on specific social and cultural factors to explain how the other aspects of social life operate. They tend to act as if the geological circumstances in which we live stretch back indefinitely into long, slow time, even if they recognize important variations across time as to which of the earth's fields of energy—such as wood, water power, peat bogs, whale oil, coal, oil, natural gas, nuclear energy, or solar power—become the resources of choice.

In an important qualification, sociocentrism soon becomes the admission that extractive capitalism and communism themselves became potent geological forces at some point—with the parties disagreeing on when these two started changing things such as drought patterns and glacier flows. This latter vision, however, is often linked—at least until recently— to the tacit presumption that planetary glacier flows, climate change, species extinctions, evolutionary turns, bacterial spread, ocean levels, and the ocean conveyor system moved on long slow time until the advent of productive systems built around carbon extraction, deforestation, CO_2 emissions, regional exploitation, and consumption abundance. The second version downplays the bumpy trajectories of self-organized planetary forcings and amplifiers.

Yet a third form—albeit also more promising than the first—is an abstract idea articulated by philosophers such as Bernard Williams. They combine the sense that the larger world is not highly predisposed to human well-being with a hesitancy to explore how the relevant planetary forces actually enter into dense imbrications with numerous aspects of social life at different historical junctures.

Consider, too, a twin of sociocentrism: human exceptionalism. In its strongest guise, it is the assumption that humans are the only intelligent and entitled beings on the planet, either because we are made in the image of an omnipotent, providential God or because we godless beings are beneficiaries of an evolutionary rupture that renders us uniquely equipped to master planetary processes. Humans are subjects—albeit usually ordered historically and hierarchically according to the degree to which they have mastered nature—and the rest of the world is composed mostly of objects.

Exceptionalism comes in several shapes and sizes, too, with some stretched out to welcome higher vertebrates as poor cousins. But most forms of exceptionalism cohere in effacing or disavowing radical entanglements human beings have with interwoven processes of multiple sorts. In order to contest it, you don't need to deny distinctiveness to human beings—with their impressive language capacities, technological achievements, scientific acumen, historical awareness, tendencies to violence, and religious proclivities. For all species have distinctive capacities and collective forms of life. You merely need to emphasize how densely entangled all human cultures are with the strivings of bacteria that enliven and debilitate their bodies, an evolutionary history that equipped them with reptile brains that form bumpy connections with the cerebral cortex, plants and animals that evolve as they enter into qualitative relations with us, shifting ocean currents that affect the environing climate, irregular glacier flows that influence land temperatures and water supplies, expanding or contracting droughts that shape the range of habitation and tendencies to feast or famine, monsoon variations that enable or disable agriculture, species extinction events that once opened a door for humans to thrive and now jeopardize the fish, bacteria, viruses, wildlife, and plants with whom we are entangled, the spread of ocean acidification that extends several of these processes, and so on and on.

Entangled humanists challenge fantasies of cultural self-sufficiency and dominance over nature that often accompany exceptionalism without always contending either that every nonhuman force in the world is also an agent—though very many are in varying ways and degrees—or insisting that care for human welfare must be sacrificed entirely to generic care for the earth itself. Rather, we are entangled with multiple and heterogeneous processes and seek to appreciate and cultivate those entanglements in ways that do not jeopardize humanity itself.

Entangled humanists enhance appreciation of multiple modes of striving and agency with which human cultures are delicately imbricated; we focus attention on racial and ethnic issues posed by the modern asymmetry between the regional sources of the triggers to galloping climate change and the regional victims; we note how class hierarchies and hierarchies of exposure to eco-risks tend to mesh in capitalist systems; and we intensify premonitions already floating around about the importance of enlarging the diversity of factors, elements, agencies, and temporalities relevant to understanding social life. Entangled humanists extend the reach of care without contending that the species life of human beings—in its vast variety of circumstances—is unimportant.[34]

Many stories of multiple gods have long appreciated such entanglements, as we have seen already in Sophocles. Moreover, not all believers in a single God are exceptionalists; nor are all Euro-American nontheists. Both of those latter traditions, however, have spawned major constituencies who do support exceptionalism. I suspect that Bernard Williams was a carrier of human exceptionalism, even as he appreciated abstractly how nonhuman forces are less favorably disposed to us than his humanist predecessors had presumed. This realist was rather unrealistic about the periodic volatility of micro and macro planetary processes. He was insufficiently attuned to entangled realism.

Others in Euro-American theo-philosophical thought, such as William James, Henri Bergson, Catherine Keller, and Alfred North Whitehead have disowned exceptionalism; the limited God they often admire is said itself to participate in complex temporalities that exceed it.[35] Another distinction between nontheists who seek to disown entanglement and those who emphasize it is also pertinent. I run with nontheistic orientations to entanglement while seeking ties of spiritual affiliation with the advocates of theo-entanglement.

Debates between those who emphasize sociocentrism and those who focus on the glories of human exceptionalism have been numerous and significant. Many explanatory reductionists fall into the first camp; interpretive critiques of reductionism into the second. But underexplored complementarities between these two debating partners tend to block awareness of how often they have both shared background assumptions about planetary gradualism. That complementarity tends to inflate a sense of generic human entitlements over nature, entitlements that in practice also devolve into privileges for a small regional minority within the human estate said to realize those entitlements most fully.

Sophocles and Mary Shelley, well before the 1980s revolution in the earth sciences, rattled such smug, self-defeating assumptions.

It is critical to address non-Euro-American modes of thought in decolonizing areas that often suffer the most today from climate change, as they also contest exceptionalism and sociocentrism.[36] It is also pertinent to review dominant Euro-American trends of thought that have supported the assumptions of sociocentrism and/or exceptionalism, as they have worked within the capacious, problematic frame of planetary gradualism. The latter traditions, indeed, block reciprocal exchanges with several non-Eurocentric cultures. Augustine, Kant, Hegel, Weber, Freud, Arendt, Rawls, Lacan, and Habermas are leading carriers of such tendencies, as Williams already suggested in his own way with respect to several of them. The *objet petit a*, for instance, is a hole at the center of the human symbolic order, not the sign of a host of planetary forces equipped with agencies, volatilities, and amplifiers of their own.

These dominant modes of European thought can also be compared to an eccentric (or minor) tradition of European thinkers who insist upon the periodic volatility of nonhuman processes, who emphasize the importance of nature/culture imbrications of diverse sorts, who invest many nonhuman actants with purpose and striving, who often enough acknowledge tragic possibility in the world, and who often embrace the sweetness of life in a world not highly predisposed to organic belonging, capitalist mastery, or communist control over nature. Hesiod, Heraclitus, Sophocles, Prodicus, Lucretius, Giordano Bruno, Spinoza, Nietzsche, Kafka, Mary Shelley, Bruno Latour, Michel Serres, James Baldwin, Donna Haraway, Catherine Keller, Gilles Deleuze, Viveiros de Castro, Jane Bennett, Lynn Margulis, and Karen Barad—in varying degrees and ways—inhabit such a minor, eccentric tradition.[37] Bernard Williams is an honorary cousin.

The Euro-American humanities and human sciences did not produce the late modern predicament of rampant climate change by themselves, of course. We/they have been, rather, rampant enablers, long too uncritical of extractive practices and the pursuit of fossil extraction, high productivity, and consumer abundance in capitalist, socialist, and communist societies, even as many in the latter two traditions exposed the economic injustices, neocolonial racism, and imperial power of advanced capitalist states.

Let's tarry a moment, then, on a pivotal group who once helped to set the geological table upon which the planetary innocence of the humanities and human sciences was set: pre-1980s earth scientists who may have unconsciously absorbed some previous theo-ontological assumptions about planetary gradualism and unwittingly contributed to the vicissitudes of the contemporary condition.

Charles Darwin and Charles Lyell—perhaps more entangled with the remains of a Constantinian story of divine omnipotence and providential history than the nontheistic theorist of evolution and the leading geologist realized—insisted in the late nineteenth century that large, planetary processes move on long, slow time. There had been mass extinctions, they admitted—conceding this much to the despised French catastrophist Cuvier whose very existence and theory revealed the possibility of other assumptions. But these shifts were gradual, the dominant theorists said, because the environments in which they occurred change very slowly. Existing gaps in the geological record, they said, would eventually be filled to confirm those assumptions.

Not until the 1980s was such an evolutionary view challenged robustly within the earth sciences themselves. The debate over that challenge then lasted a long decade before the punctuationists won.[38] The humanities and human sciences are still—though there are now numerous shining exceptions—catching up with this veritable revolution in the planetary sciences.[39] Even while vehemently opposing climate denialism, many humanists still inhale fumes from a gradualist perspective burned out decades ago in the earth sciences. That time lag does not merely make many slide over previous planetary events with severe consequences of their own; it underplays how capitalist triggers of climate change today become imbricated with multiple amplifiers that can induce climate, glacier, species, and ocean conveyor changes that greatly exceed the force of the triggers.

To challenge gradualism, you need to contest the quaint idea of David Hume that correlation never means causation, and you also need to proceed well beyond the boundaries of efficient causality. Now you explore how heterogeneous agencies and forces of multiple types periodically both infuse and impinge upon one another. A huge volcanic eruption sets off a series of heterogeneous relays and infusions between the dust in the stratosphere, climate, crop failures, bacterial change, plagues, famine, refugee drives, and social unrest. That poses a better image to start with than either sociocentrism or human exceptionalism.

We now know of course that there have been several mass species extinction events before humans reached high population levels. But climate has also fluctuated radically over even the last 100,000 years. Luis Alvarez, Stephen Jay Gould, Richard B. Alley, Naomi Oreskes, Michael Benton, Jan Zalasiewicz, Wally Broecker, and James Hansen are merely a few in the earth sciences who have fomented this veritable revolution.[40] My counter-factual hunch is that if they had had closer access to eccentric traditions of Western thought—including Hesiod, Heraclitus, Sophocles, Lucretius, Mary Shelley, and Nietzsche—they might have articulated and tested such hypotheses earlier. Stephen Jay Gould may concur, given his belated recognition that his own theory of punctuated equilibrium was preceded a century earlier by Nietzsche, the philologist and philosopher who was the Sophocles of the nineteenth century.[41]

It is insufficient (if highly pertinent) to admit that state capitalism, socialism, and communism became potent geological forces in the nineteenth and twentieth centuries—unwittingly at first and then with increasing knowledge—damaging a larger set of world regional ecologies and intensifying internal zones of exploitation. It is, moreover, misleading to counter those images with an organic story of nature, in which things would quickly return to a benign state if only the human imprint on the planet were reduced. That latter story overlooks how current capitalist climate triggers set a series of cascading amplifiers into motion that may not be reversed for centuries.

It is essential, then, to study how the geological impacts of societies of extraction, production and consumer abundance—amid the radical regional, race, and class inequalities and sacrifices produced by the march of progress—intersect with potent planetary amplifiers that create large gaps between civilizational triggers and the cascading processes that ensue.

To be an entangled humanist with eco-concern today is to extend the reach of social inquiry and care beyond the provincial parameters of sociocentrism, planetary gradualism, humanist exceptionalism, and linear time. Kant's harmonious division between the subjective human faculties has been blown away by a series of wildfires and dust storms. Freud's reduction of the Oedipus story to an Oedipus complex has been infected by plagues and droughts—elemental features of existence already appreciated by the wise Sophocles. Bacteria and viruses now travel rapidly on global human transportation systems.

Oedipus found out he was hunting himself; perhaps Victor Frankenstein eventually suspected the same thing about himself. We now see that in advanced capitalist states we have been stalking ourselves, too, as we create a monster that now grows through its own momentum.

We will address the rocky relations between climate forcings, noncyclical drivers, capitalist triggers, and planetary amplifiers in the next essay. For now, perhaps, it is timely to hope that new voices approaching the poetic powers of Sophocles and Mary Shelley will pull more people out of the funk in which they pretend that resistance to climate denialism suffices. The scourge of climate denialism has in fact had two disastrous effects. It has, first, delayed responses in the United States above all to an accelerating condition. It has, second, discouraged those who might be called climate casualists from coming to terms more urgently with heterogeneous connections and cascading processes through which the acceleration of climate change surges today.

Two

The Anthropocene as Abstract Machine

To inhabit the geological era recently known as the Anthropocene is not to live during a time when—as if flouting millions of years of long, slow change in oceans, species evolution, climate, glaciers, and deserts—humanity writ large suddenly became a geological force. Such a statement asserts two mistakes: the assumption of planetary gradualism in itself with which it starts and the charge of generic human responsibility with which it closes. Geology, paleontology, oceanography, glaciology, and other sciences—starting as late as the 1980s—finally exploded the story of planetary gradualism that had informed the nineteenth-century geologist Lyell and the evolutionary theorist Darwin. It is an interesting question to pose: What kind of metaphysical and cosmological assumptions in Christian providentialism and its remainders in secular thought encouraged such sciences to take so long? Unfortunately, however, despite recent changes in the earth sciences, the remains of scientific gradualism continue to haunt the humanities, the social sciences, and democratic citizenship.

Second assumption: humanity did not become a geological force in the modern era. Rather, state capitalism, socialism, and communism, organized around internally differentiated priorities of fossil extraction, productivism, and consumption abundance, became major geological forces by dint of their dominant institutionalizations and existential priorities. They imposed new, rapidly accelerating burdens and injuries on racially defined constituencies, the lower classes, and several regions outside the centers of extractive capitalism. So much, so obvious, though the corrections do require adjustments in the way the term "Anthropocene" was introduced by geologists.

If you interrogated the five great mass extinction events that occurred before these recent systems of political economy triumphed, it would also become clear how capitalism and the rest are not the sole geological forces of rapid, deep change today either—in contrast to the lingering assumption in the humanities that planetary forces moved on long slow time on their own until the advent of capitalism. These modern political economies, rather, spawn climate triggers that can become inflated or dampened by a variety of planetary forcings and self-organizing amplifiers; the latter often spawn cascading processes with results that vastly exceed the impetus that triggered them. We need a concept of cascading causality to explore multiple, intersecting trajectories with various degrees of agency. Not all planetary forces are agents, in the sense of exuding at least some capacity to strive, feel, and, in conjunction with other forces, periodically bring something new into the world. But blind forces and purposive agents of different sorts do interact in the Anthropocene—as they did long before it emerged.

Gilles Deleuze and Félix Guattari did not examine the Anthropocene in relation to capitalist and communist practices of productivism. Guattari's *The Three Ecologies*, written in 1986, did explore how three eco-registers— the environmental, the social, and the mental—have reverberated back and forth to create eco-neglect.[1] And he already identified Donald Trump as a ruthless agent. But Guattari did not focus on the volatility of planetary processes themselves in that book.

Deleuze and Guattari (D&G) together, however, opened a door to such examinations through introduction of a series of concepts that emphasize the repeated salience of human/nonhuman imbrications in history and the ways diverse human cultural practices are profoundly entangled with a host of nonhuman forces and agencies with diverse speeds, capacities, and trajectories of their own. Many components of the latter, again, display variable strivings and agentic capacities, capacities that challenge together the sufficiency of human exceptionalism, sociocentrism, cultural internalism, and planetary gradualism that heretofore graced much of Euro-American philosophy, the humanities, and social sciences.

Moreover, D&G's appreciation of the recurrent volatility of such imbrications may challenge in advance neoliberal, liberal, socialist, or communist images of an ideal future, whenever any of those ideals is adamantly committed to expanding productivity and economic growth. Accelerating minoritization of the world and of planetary volatility—two trends that D&G found to be intertwined—generate the need to rethink both dominant modes of explanation and the social ideals within which contending explanatory traditions have been embroiled. Not a world without ideals, then, but ideals better adjusted to the galloping pace and decentering powers of the Anthropocene.

Several D&G concepts are pertinent to the inquiry in question. One key pair they introduce—smooth and striated space—is critical. A few paradigms of smooth space are oceans, deserts, glaciers, mountain ranges, the atmosphere, mist, creative thinking, the stratosphere, steppes, and prairies. Several smooth spaces expand or contract over time, making huge differences to possibilities of life in and around them. Certainly, each is susceptible to new practices of striation that would organize and define it more sharply. The introduction of longitude and latitude onto ocean maps is a modest example of striation. So is the division of prairie land into territories marked by moats, river borders, passport controls, county divisions, racial divisions, state bureaucracies, surveillance systems, class hierarchies, highway systems, and/or territorial walls.

The most critical thing for our purposes in the D&G exploration of differences, intersections, and transitions between smooth and striated space is how the two adventurers command attention to the shifting character and pertinence of such large expanses, flows, and processes. Their interventions compel social thinkers to address the shifting density and size of drought zones, monsoons, ocean currents, desertification, rates of glacier flow, hurricanes, atmospheric composition, and so forth, since all of them are intertwined with the waxing and waning of human and nonhuman life on the planet. D&G thus introduce several categories that cut off sociocentrism at the pass—the latter being the quaint idea that key social processes can be explained almost solely by reference to more basic social processes. Intense debates within sociocentrism, while important, also distract attention from a complementarity that binds the debating partners together.

When you think of how various planetary processes themselves slide and bump into shifting mixtures of social life, several other D&G concepts present themselves as candidates too. Assemblage, rhizome, multiplicity, body without organs, plane of composition, and abstract machine pop up for consideration. A rhizome, for instance, consists of multiple energies, openings, and trajectories through which numerous lines of flight and heterogeneous connections between disparate entities generate new formations not previously in motion. Not bad. The concept of an assemblage is rather promising too, designed as it is to displace tired old debates between the notion of the preformed individual and the holistic organism. An assemblage is composed of multiple, partly open and heterogeneous constituents that maintain self-stability for a determinate period.

Symbiogenesis in evolution involves an assemblage, say, between the entry of new gut bacteria and the neuronal organization of a change in a species, or, say, when viruses enter the human germ line to introduce a new change through horizontal gene transfer. Theories of horizontal modes of evolution are rapidly overtaking the sense of sufficiency in the old vertical, treelike stories, adding crucial horizontal flows to the vertical processes also in play. Another type of assemblage consists of disparate constituencies that gather together to energize a new social movement, each adjusting some of its contours to the others. The notion of assemblage plays up ideas of intersecting constituents and morphing trajectories over those of fixed configurations and structures, even while it appreciates the importance of specific modes of stabilization. It complicates the notion of "is" and the grammatical sufficiency of sentences organized around the subject/predicate form. It folds a notion of bumpy temporalities into the middle of life, being, and inquiry.

But I suspect the idea of an abstract machine may do even more work to rethink the Anthropocene, partly because of its emphasis on fecund processes that both involve and exceed human powers and partly because of its focus on imbrications between elements of diverse types in processes of formation, consolidation, and deconsolidation. A couple of things D&G say about abstract machines are relevant, even if that concept may need a bit of additional work to speak to the Anthropocene. Abstract machines "are defined by the fourth aspect of assemblages, in other words, the cutting edges of decoding and deterritorialization. . . . Therefore they make the territorial assemblage open onto something else, assemblages of another type, the molecular, the cosmic: they constitute becomings." And "each abstract machine can be considered a 'plateau' of variation."[2] An abstract machine thus composes heterogeneous temporalities that are self-organizing to various degrees. The earth itself is an abstract machine: it "asserts its own powers of deterritorialization, its lines of flight, its smooth spaces that live and blaze their way for a new earth."[3]

My usage may not entirely conform to definitions these wanderers sometimes give, however, in that the planetary machine to be mapped here is a formation itself rather than being merely—as they sometimes suggest—preliminary to other formations.[4] So I will work upon the notion a bit to help trace the accelerating powers of the Anthropocene. They did not really explore the latter condition to my knowledge, and, anyway, these two philosophers of the event invite you to adapt their notions to diverse times and processes.

An abstract machine, in the sense deployed here, includes moving, morphing planetary complexes that exceed the power of the ensemble of forces and agencies that constitute it. It is machinic (rather than strictly mechanistic, cybernetic, or organic) in that it evolves new speeds and powers as it draws energy from earthquakes, capitalist emissions, ocean currents, volcanoes, methane bursts, microbes, and the sun to cut into prior stabilizations; planetary (in this instance) in that it imposes asymmetrical regional, racial, class, and species consequences for living beings on the face of the earth; abstract in the sense that it is irreducible to the multitude of forcings and agencies that compose it such as, say, capitalism, white evangelicalism, techno-scientific formations, imperial patterns of trade and finance, tectonic plates, ressentiment, species evolution, viral and bacterial flows, desert advances, ocean currents, acidification, and glacier flows; and it is complex in the sense that the heterogeneous forces that compose it both impinge upon each other and periodically infuse one another to some degree to endow the self-organizing machine with evolving shapes, speeds, and trajectories.

Capitalism and the Anthropocene

I understand, with D&G, capitalism to be composed by a shifting axiomatic that exceeds both a determinate mode of production and the rationality of impersonal market processes. The axiomatic, in its shifting shapes, enables some activities, constrains others, and captures yet others. Such an image of capitalism outstrips every mode of economism, partly because it includes shifting spiritualities that infuse institutions of production, investment, governance, class struggle, and consumption, partly because this image focuses on the emissions that change climate, and partly because capitalism today faces planetary forces with powers of self-amplification that intrude into it in multifarious ways. While an axiomatic enables and constrains institutional processes that combine unevenly together to form a capitalist regime, the regime often finds itself searching and groping in the dark as new events unfold or erupt. It is thus never exempt from creative practices of politics that infuse its institutions and pursuits. Capitalism is a shape-shifting power formation both influencing and exceeded by volatile planetary forces bound to its rocky history and destiny.

A capitalist axiomatic of enablement and constraint may consist, in one mode, of private ownership and pursuit of profit, a focus on fossil fuel extraction, a commodity form of consumption, labor pushed kicking and screaming toward the commodity form, states organized as servants and/or regulators of the axiomatic, and banks with varying degrees of independence. These old axioms can then be stretched or contracted to foster real temporal and regional diversities within different forms of capitalism writ large. Some variations take the form of democratic capitalism in which competing parties shuffle between enthusiastically subordinating themselves to the vicissitudes of the axiomatic and regulating it to protect workers, consumers, public goods, and nonhuman species; fascist capitalism in which a dictatorial party mobilizes a couple of intense factions to guide private capital and to exercise terror, surveillance, and racist control over others; Keynesian capitalism in which unions acquire increased institutional power and in which a social net for workers, the poor, the old, the disabled, and the infirm is established by the state; or neoliberal capitalism in which democracy becomes thinned out, corporate regulations are stripped, state subsidies for capital flourish, and a myth (or overcoding) of market rationality is invoked to justify these practices.

Under conditions of stress, neoliberal capitalism can morph toward fascist capitalism, as occurred after the Great Depression in several states and as a host of new social movements drive to accomplish today in the U.S., Poland, Hungary, Austria, Turkey, Brazil, and Italy. The racial dog whistles and thinly denied white triumphalism that marked neoliberalism now become bullhorns. Big lies, aggressive nationalism, voter suppression, corruption of courts, intelligence agencies, and judicial policies, harsh policing of territorial borders, market testing of new modes of cruelty, and media intimidation now attain new heights of intensity. The big-lie scenario plays an important role in such regimes, in which leaders both dramatize false accusations against others to mobilize a base and disclose tells about themselves in doing so. Think, for instance, of how Donald Trump's lies about climate change as a hoax, the secret governance by a deep state, the critique of a Supreme Court nominee as mob rule, and his opponents as authors of con jobs. This guy, in turn, clearly propagates an anti–climate change hoax, has a history of tax evasion and relations with mobsters, seeks to install a deep state to serve him, and has regularly pursued con jobs in his real estate business. The double purpose of such lies is to muddy the waters of charges brought against him while also demeaning those who strive to hold him accountable.[5]

Fascism does not necessarily mean the end of formal public elections; it can mean their transfiguration into authoritarian plebiscites through Big Lies, selective voter suppression, crony courts to limit dissident activism, close alliances with manipulative media outlets, selective economic squeezes, sharp definition of foreign adversaries, virulent propagation of scapegoats held responsible for economic squeezes and existential anxieties, and the strategic use of police and intelligence agencies to target and compromise specific constituencies. In the United States, African Americans, independent women, Muslims, Mexicans, the media, and the professoriate are popular targets partly because such constituencies can be demeaned, blamed, and attacked as scapegoats in ways that do not require deep reforms of neoliberal capitalism and partly because several of these constituencies provide sites of resistance to aspirational fascism.

The key connections between extractive capitalism, the galloping Anthropocene, and new fascist movements in old democratic states are perhaps these: First, climate warming, drought, stuttering monsoons, glacier melts, wildfires, extreme storms, and so on press upon vulnerable and exploited regions, increasing pressure for civil wars and forced migrations. The resulting racialized refugee pressures upon old capitalist states create happy hunting grounds for the purveyors of aspirational fascism in those regimes, as the latter call for a pure white nation, close ties to strongmen in other states, intimidation of internal critics, aggressive foreign policies, and territorial walls. Second, as those flames are fanned by aspirational fascists—with Donald Trump leading the way in America—white workers and the lower middle class in deindustrialized zones are told that only by returning to the old days of fossil fuel extraction, steel and automobile production, and white triumphalism can they hope to regain the levels of entitlement acquired precariously in the 1950s and 1960s. Trump's focus on coal workers here is revealing, since they are icons of the old white working class. This combination pulls some to embrace climate denialism and to support an authoritarian leader; it encourages others (particularly in white upper middle and donor classes) to tolerate and fund such expressions of public belief to fend off challenges from the left.[6] Sometimes the resulting ambivalence between embrace and tolerance finds expression in the same selves and constituencies.[7] White triumphalism and climate denialism, nonetheless, support one another today, in part because it will indeed take radical reform of dominant practices over a single decade to respond to the perils of the Anthropocene.

The acceleration of the Anthropocene, when neglected, is thus closely linked to the rise of fascist pressures in old capitalist states. Indeed, the longer old capitalist states delay in reconstituting themselves to reduce the adverse effects of rapid climate change, the more the danger of fascism grows.

Accelerationism—in its left-wing expressions—is the contemporary claim that the only way to respond to neoliberal capitalism today is to accelerate its own tendencies to self-destruction and austerity until it collapses from its own contradictions.[8] The frustrations pushing some critics on the left into accelerationism are understandable. But I note that left-wing proponents of accelerationism tend to underplay the acceleration of the Anthropocene itself that is well underway. If they did attend to it, it is doubtful that they would be able to pretend that a new, just society would emerge out of quickening the wreckage of the old. For the Anthropocene, by then, would have reached such a point of devastation that it would be too late to respond to it in a just way. Even without that fundamental consideration, accelerationists discount too much the class, race, and regional suffering that acceleration brings with it. The biggest danger facing the ideology of accelerationism is not merely the extension of neoliberal capitalism, it is that the latter will morph into new modes of fascist capitalism.

That is why I do not support accelerationism, but rather a series of rapid, positive interim policies and democratic practices to press current capitalist states, first, beyond extractive capitalism and, second, beyond the class organization of acquisitive desires joined to the differential ability of people in different subject positions to fulfill them. That is one reason an initial focus on reshaping the infrastructure and ethos of consumption is so important today. We point toward an egalitarian, socialist, pluralist democracy that works to reduce existing pressures to consume, even though we know that this agenda, too, has become a long shot in today's world.[9] Today, given the urgency of time, it assumes the character of an improbable necessity.

Capitalism, with its endemic pressures to expand growth, exploit nature, workers, and consumers, extend income and wealth hierarchies, generate crises, and deploy fossil fuels thus plays a crucial role in the advance of the Anthropocene. But other forces also make signal contributions to its trajectory and speed. Indeed, capitalist states vary significantly among themselves in the extent to which they continue on the extractive course. The United States—the home of a virulent evangelical/neoliberal assemblage that has been morphing toward aspirational fascism—pursues a highly destructive course. Indeed, white evangelicalism became a new axiom added to U.S. capitalism in the 1980s, disclosing again how some axioms of capitalism are not economistic in shape.

How has this assemblage between evangelicals and neoliberals worked? White evangelicals foment an accusatory spirituality toward nonwhites, ecologists, the media, migration, independent women, decolonial regimes, and intellectuals, as they often construe the market to be a vehicle of God's providence and the democratic state to be a bureaucratic titan. Neoliberals exude a spirituality of hubris over workers and nature, treating both as deposits of resources for use. They insist that a self-organizing privately incorporated market would lift all boats and regulate itself rationally if only it were left free to roar. Each of these two constituencies then folds aspects of the spiritual temper of the other into its own mode of politics. The result is a politics of accusatory hubris whenever obstacles to realization of the impossible future projected become more visible. And, indeed, during the Anthropocene obstacles to realization of the future officially projected do become increasingly severe. The gap between the future the evangelical/capitalist machine demands and its capacity to deliver on that future keeps growing, creating space for new intensities of fascist accusation, mobilization, and imposition. For example, oil companies now face a twenty-year time gap between the time a deep-water or fracking project starts and the day it delivers a market return. So fossil fuel companies must forge alliances with the state to make sure the future is there when the product is ready for delivery. Donald Trump's drive to reduce regulated gasoline mileage in vehicles, despite the health and climate consequences of that action, can be understood as another tactic to secure by state action the future needed by oil companies. Neoliberalism always pursues a large, supportive state, only one with very different priorities from, say, a social democratic state.

Put another way, as the evangelical/neoliberal machine slides or gallops closer to an embrace of fascist capitalism, climate denialism and casualism readily become axioms of that assemblage. The slide of neoliberalism down this incline can be seen in Republican Party expansive views of presidential sovereignty, its tolerance of a territorial wall, its retreat from free trade, its refusals to criticize presidential racism, its readiness to embrace huge deficits to gain tax breaks for the rich, its willingness to short circuit a whole series of established congressional norms to appoint an aggressive judge, and its readiness to participate in cover-ups of Trump's multifaceted conspiracy with Russia to corrupt a democratic election.

Other capitalist countries such as Chile, Germany, Japan, and Denmark are both capitalistic and less stuck on such destructive eco-paths. China sometimes moves in this direction too. Capitalism, writ large, is a major force in the Anthropocene, then, but it is neither its only agentic force nor uniform across states in its destructive tendencies.

The Late Antique Little Ice Machine

We can discern more closely how capitalism is exceeded by the climate dynamic to which it makes a major contribution by attending to other times when climate change was in play before either state capitalism or state communism existed. We need not turn merely to the period 250 million years ago when 90 percent of life was wiped out, or 66 million years ago when 50 percent of life was extinguished, though the cascading, nonhuman processes through which these two mass extinctions unfolded are highly pertinent to the trajectory taken by the current planetary machine. We can look closer at hand to the fall of Rome.

According to Kyle Harper, in *The Fate of Rome*, the Roman Climate Optimum lasted from about 200 BCE to about 150 CE; that period was highly suitable for lavish crops, population growth, and the takeoff of imperial expansion.[10] Complex modes of governance, enlarged patterns of trade, and dominance over the Mediterranean basin were consolidated during the Roman Climate Optimum. The Late Antique Little Ice Age—a very recently discovered and named climate machine—started later and coalesced with the devastating plagues induced by the unwitting importation of black rats and fleas from the East through consolidation of new trading routes.[11] These two events further weakened the empire. Such bacterial, insect, animal, and climate incursions into the empire, of course, mean that a purely hermeneutic or sociocentric approach to the decline of Rome cannot suffice; the participants themselves had little idea of the sources of the plague and no idea of the source of the climate change that later wreaked such devastations. They often sought the sources in divine judgments and decisions.

Indeed, the rapid growth of Constantinian Christianity in Rome correlates loosely, first, with the dates of pestilence and, second, with climate change, perhaps in part because that version of Christianity could blame the widespread suffering on the weakness of the pagan gods, the desert of pagan Rome (a Second Coming was promised), and the capacity of an omnipotent God to surpass the two phenomena through promise of a blissful afterlife to deserving believers. In 200 CE there were hardly any Christians in Rome. By 300 CE there "had been a staggering change."[12]

Key here are the words "omnipotent" and "salvational," for that is the hegemonic spiritual version of Christianity that invaded the empire. "The natural catastrophes of the sixth century induced one of the greatest mood swings in human history. The occlusion of the sun, the rattling of the earth, and the advent of world-wide plague stoked the fires of eschatological expectation across the Christian world and beyond."[13] We discern here a Christian/imperial complex that underlines recurrent connections between the spiritual ethos of a time, shifting planetary conditions, and the shape of a regime.

It is thus pertinent to note how one version of Christianity triumphed over other versions rattling around during this period. The Constantinian doctrine of an omnipotent, sovereign, salvational God supported the imperial Roman doctrine of the emperor as unquestioned ruler. The injunction was to obey both the sovereign God and the sovereign emperor. There were certainly other versions of Christianity—some laden with different potentialities—but that is the version Constantine consolidated.

As Catherine Keller and Catherine Nixey combine from two different perspectives to show, the rapid conversion of more and more "pagans" in Rome—a derogatory term invented to describe diverse non-Christian faiths as inferior and idolatrous—was accompanied by advances in state dogmatism and by the widely dispersed destruction of pagan temples and statues by violent, roving monks. Rampaging monks would raid old temples in Egypt, Syria, Rome, and Greece, defacing pagan statues and temples, injuring or killing worshippers, and collecting the stones liberated to use for Christian edifices—with the triumphant new uses often engraved as carvings over the old etchings. Triumphalism could now be signified directly as the faithful trod upon old, defaced pagan stones.

By the time Justinian imposed an edict in 399 CE commanding all members of the empire to become (Constaninian) Christians and to destroy pagan symbols, the process of Roman Christianization was well in hand. So planetary body blows, especially plagues, combined with growing existential anxieties and coercive pressures to support a rapid transition to that version of Christianity—making it difficult for historians today to determine the relative weight to give to each set of pressures.[14]

Did the climate and plague shocks of the day accentuate a sense of the shaky place of the human estate in the cosmos itself? If so, Constantinian Christianity was now available to absorb that anxiety and to transfigure it into obeisance to a sovereign God who promised the possibility of eternal salvation.

These spiritual forces coalesced with other forces, as when invading Huns from drought-stricken zones to the East pressed retreating Goths to increase their pressure on the Roman state. A key point here is that the Romans did not know quite what was happening: a conjunction of disparate pressures from multiple sites converged upon them, including ruling dictates, black rats, plagues, existential anxieties, roving monks, nomadic pressures, and, soon, intensification of a new ice age machine. Some of those sources were cloaked in mystery. "The Plague of Justinian was the greatest mortality event up to that point in human history . . . and the Late Antique Little Ice Age was a regime as inhospitable to the political project of the Roman Empire as the Climate Optimum had once been favorable to the great pope's distant ancestors."[15]

How, though, did the Late Antique Little Ice Age acquire momentum in 536 CE and surge until around 545, creating cold years that outstripped the now better-known Little Ice Age that reached its peak in the seventeenth century? Recent geological, ice core, isotope, chronicle, and tree-ring evidence suggests that the Late Antique Little Ice Age was intensified by a massive volcanic eruption in 536 CE that released massive amounts of sulfur into the stratosphere. This shift in climate was bolstered by a cyclical sun dimming already underway and, soon thereafter, by another huge tropical volcanic eruption that finished it off. The next great plague correlated with these events.

These multiple whammies did not by themselves cause the collapse of Rome—or, better, its devolution into a more decentralized medieval era. Rather, "these harsh years quietly added stress to an imperial order already stressed."[16] Harper folds volcanic eruptions, sun dimming, climate, plagues, emperor impositions, imported rats, infected fleas, and inflated existential anxieties into yet other forces to explain the fate of Rome.

Planetary/cultural shifts of importance are seldom reducible to singular causes, or even to an ensemble of efficient causes. The elements of a cascading ensemble penetrate into each other as they also impinge upon one another in a world made up of heterogeneous entities with varying degrees of porosity and efficacious power.

Once the Late Antique Little Ice Age and accompanying plagues burst forth, the regime encountered a variety of human and nonhuman amplifiers that helped the machine to accelerate and Rome to become further weakened. For example, the climate pressure on crops encouraged further deforestation to add new soil for cultivation, perhaps raising the temperature slightly but also increasing tendencies to drought. And, again, climate pressures facing nomadic tribes promoted pressures to intensify their own drives against Rome. Those powerful processes intersected with a series of loosely intercoded contingencies, such as overextension of the empire, military adventurism, trade routes that drew rats and fleas with them, the destruction of republicanism, nomadic invasions, and internal corruption.

One thing to note today is how earlier accounts of the rise and fall of Rome did not stress the role of the Roman Climate Optimum or the Late Antique Little Ice Age, though the plagues were noted. Some Roman chroniclers themselves had complained about changes in climate, but modern historians apparently did not emphasize these happenings, perhaps because they were unaware of the previous history of periodic and deep climate changes, some of which were rapid. These cultural historians may have unconsciously inhaled the fumes of nineteenth- and twentieth-century sciences of geology, climatology, and paleontology that themselves were still stuck in the grooves of planetary gradualism or uniformitarianism.

Except for a few minor voices, stories of planetary gradualism only began to break in the major earth sciences after the discovery in 1980 by Luis Alvarez of the great asteroid 66 million years ago that instigated a huge, rapid mass extinction. It took another long decade before the new planetary story was widely digested in the earth sciences and linked to earlier deep changes in planetary trajectories.[17] And, again, longer yet before Euro-American philosophy, the humanities, and the social sciences really began to internalize these findings.

One more thing before we depart Rome. As Catherine Keller argues in *Political Theology of the Earth*, it is pertinent to attend to a series of historical relays and reverberations between the Roman Church's insistence that God created the world from nothing, the parallel Constantine draws between a sovereign God above time and an emperor who rules his subjects without question, the unity soon demanded between empire and that Christian faith by Justinian, the later rise of Calvinism, the quest by the Church of England to ground Christianity in an Anglo-Saxon race, the transfiguration of theologies of divine omnipotence by Carl Schmitt into a secular doctrine in which the state sovereign becomes he who decides, white evangelical demands in America for identity between Constantinian doctrine and the shape of a white Christian nation, capitalist firms that demand authoritarian controls over workers, and fascist movements demanding sovereign, unquestioned rule over an entire people. When Stephen Miller, the assistant to Donald Trump, told the American people early in Trump's term that they would soon realize that the sovereign decisions of the president could not be questioned, he was drawing upon a long, checkered tradition of such sovereign doctrines.

When Donald Trump expressed his admiration for how the subjects of Kim Jong-un snap to attention when Kim enters the room, he conveyed his attraction to a fascist doctrine of sovereignty. The loose but real relays between divine omnipotence, human exceptionalism, American exceptionalism, racial exceptionalism, and sovereign exceptionalism are thus worthy of critical attention.

This is certainly not to say that there is a single, straight line running necessarily from the first pattern of insistence to later assertions of sovereign entitlement. These are, rather, loose cultural lineages of association, inspiration, and reverberation. Some of these forces and associations may dissipate for a while and then rise in new ways under conditions of stress. Under the contemporary situation of existential stress—when people worry again about the shaky place of human life in the cosmos—old patterns of insistence floating around in several doctrines, spiritualities, and institutions readily find new modes of dramatization. The doctrine of papal absolutism is one of those old doctrines; the insistence upon authoritarian control within contemporary corporations is another; the strictness of military discipline yet another. Such associations enable a secular, authoritarian thinker such as Carl Schmitt to draw inspiration from the Constantinian doctrine as he transfers it to the more ugly aspirations of a Nazi leader. Such a transfiguration can attract larger constituencies under stress, if it already finds selective expression in churches, returning war veterans, military discipline, corporations, state doctrines, action films, frustrated workers, and aspiring leaders.

That is why those who are democrats, pluralists, egalitarians, ecologists, and critics of totalist claims to sovereignty must also draw sustenance today from countertraditions within and outside Judaism and Christianity. The minor European traditions available range from those that read the very genesis of the world through a God who worked upon bubbling materials already there, to the life of Jesus as a nonsovereign source of inspiration, through the story by the early Roman philosopher Lucretius of how the world evolves without divine guidance, to the unorthodox thought of Spinoza, through those who detect powers of self-organization in the evolution of the earth and species change, to modern process philosophies, through ecologically attentive notions of the Anthropocene as an abstract machine irreducible to a single sovereign authority. It is important today to attend to multiple theological and philosophical sources through which absolute sovereignty is challenged and eco-egalitarian, pluralist messages of activism find ample room for expression.

This last constellation, too, expresses a loose historical assemblage of minor traditions working back and forth upon one another, as they resist the singular hegemony of the Constantinian tradition and its secular partners. If and as Constantinians and their secular kissing cousins concede, without existential resentment, that their theo-cosmology is one contestable creed in a world of multiple creeds, they too can join the cross-regional, pluralist assemblages of politics needed today. That, indeed, is why so many Catholics and non-Catholics today evince respect for, and invest hope in, Pope Francis—and why we resist those drives to get rid of him.[18] Non-Constantinian traditions, indeed—that is, minor Euro-American spiritual traditions—may also be better equipped to enter into exploratory exchanges with a variety of indigenous traditions, Hinduism, Buddhism, and Islam, as recent work emanating from minor Euro-American traditions shows.[19]

Today, massive capitalist CO_2 emissions combine with deforestation processes and agribusiness methane releases to trigger a host of planetary amplifiers, some of which have also been triggered by nonhuman events earlier in planetary history. As we assess these bumpy imbrications, we not only need to think about the diverse designs and shapes capitalism has assumed—neoliberal, Keynesian, liberal, and fascistic among them—but several other nineteenth- and twentieth-century ideals contending against capitalism may also need selective reconstitution. They, too, were anchored in fossil extraction, future projections of high collective productivity, and expanding levels of collective consumption. Several nineteenth-and twentieth-century images point toward contending promises of a smooth future clustered around tacit assumptions of nature's gradualism, beneficence, regularity, and susceptibility to mastery. These also embody attempts to dehistoricize the temporal trajectories that constitute nature.

The danger of fascism now is bound immediately to cultural resentment in several old capitalist states against growing refugee pressures, some of which will accelerate due to the close relation between growing regional droughts and civil wars. A deep, longer-range source of danger is lodged in the fact that the future promises extractive capitalism advances to maintain its legitimacy are based upon desperately protected assumptions and institutionalized imperatives deeply at odds with acceleration of the Anthropocene. The demise of the doctrine of planetary gradualism stirs up a dust storm of denialism among neoliberal capitalists and many white working-class followers desperate to improve their own precarious standing in a world in which not enough others speak closely to those very insecurities. Sometimes the demise of planetary gradualism freezes critical intellectuals in place too, as we realize we must rethink the counterideals that have inspired us and hesitate to do so.

Late modern capitalism, if or when it loses the democratic practices that have often been entangled with it, becomes fascism. That is so in part because drives to keep the capitalist machine going during difficult times among a populace that had heretofore internalized free speech, citizen social movements, open elections, and a critical media now require more state repression and intense mobilization of deindustrialized constituencies to keep the dissidents under wraps. Call critics and dissenters a mob to cover up the mobster mentality governing the attempt to dismantle democracy. The old cruelties of neoliberal capitalism now morph into aspirational fascism, sometimes haunting a residual faction within liberalism itself that had been too soft on neoliberalism.

Trump, sovereign walls, growing refugee pressures, militaristic policies, the marketing of new extensions of cruelty against scapegoats, the mobilization of portions of the white working and middle class into a neofascist coalition, and belligerent neglect of climate change form an assemblage with interfaces that now work back and forth upon each other. However, an opposing dynamic is in play too: democratic energies that strive to tame capitalism rapidly through interim policies, fight off climate denialism, become much more egalitarian, and rise above the assumption of climate parallelism. This recipe provides the most promising way to defeat fascist movements of reaction.

We can now perhaps draw these threads together by explaining why neither the Anthropocene as a unique planetary configuration nor the theme of the Capitalocene may be quite up to performing the functions it is called upon to serve today. The focus now is on the latter.

In an impressive and provocative book, Jason Moore calls upon us to replace the theme of the Anthropocene with the Capitalocene.[20] The former label is too generic; the new term allows us to concentrate upon how a new political economy—capitalism—became a major geological force for the first time in history. Moore then shows how, to sustain its patterns of growth under unfavorable conditions, advanced capitalist states have been pressed to create "cheap natures" through high-tech inventions to reduce costs of production and maintain profits. So far, so illuminating and pertinent. Nonetheless, for a series of reasons, I find the idea of the Capitalocene to overreach, to underexplain, and perhaps to lure its proponents toward an ideal of productive communism also in need of overhaul. Here are some considerations that incline me in that direction.

First, as already noted, noncapitalist regimes have also periodically faced deep and sometimes rapid climate change. Some have even made a difference themselves to the conditions they face. Extensive patterns of deforestation during the Medieval Warm Period provide one example. So does Rome and, before it, Amerindian life in the American Southwest and the Mayan Empire during the Medieval Warming Period. Extractive capitalism is not unique in this regard, though its role as a powerful geological force is unmatched.

Second, the existential orientations that infuse and inform the institutions of a political economy must form part of any analysis of it. Economism is never sufficient to political economy, capitalist or otherwise. To invoke yet another example, the diffusion of deep cynicism in Soviet institutions of planning, management, and work had something to do with the demise of that regime. The emergence of an evangelical/neoliberal resonance machine in America today helps to bring the same point out; it helps to explain why this particular mode of capitalism is particularly tempted by the conjunction of racism, misogyny, and climate denialism. Migration pressures upon Europe today have altered the spiritual ethos inside those institutions as well. Rome, too, involved movements rolling back and forth between the changing shape of empire, sources of rapid climate change, and spiritual shifts in a regime as more and more people worried again about the shaky place of the human estate in a changing world.

Third, any focus on the Capitalocene as a unique configuration could tend to draw attention away from the pertinence to today of numerous other times when radical shifts in climate, oceans, glacier flows, drought, monsoons and so on occurred on their own, well before the Holocene, capitalism, or even the emergence of human life. The way these forcings, drivers, triggers, and amplifiers worked upon each had profound effects upon species life in those times and places. Their dynamics in those times and places also can teach us a lot about what is happening today during the hegemony of capitalism.[21] We don't need to locate a Golden Spike in history at which capitalism and the Capitalocene converged: we need to trace a series of convoluted exchanges between volatile planetary forces and the shifting character of political economies. In short, the theme of the Capitalocene may edge too close to the story of planetary gradualism before the advent of capitalism.

Fourth, as already established, capitalism assumes many diverse shapes. Some are more amenable to radical reform and the pursuit of sustainability than others. Keynesianism, neoliberalism, the evangelical/neoliberal machine, social democracies breaking extractivist cultures, and fascist capitalism tied to repression of minorities and the radical defilement of nature all embody forms of the capitalist problematic. Some are more amenable to radical reform than others. The generic term "capitalism" may be too abstract for the issues that engage us, though Moore senses this point as well.

Fifth, most nineteenth- and twentieth-century Euro-American ideals—including Keynesianism, neoliberalism, the evangelical/neoliberal machine, liberalism, socialism, and communism—have been organized around priorities of fossil extraction, productivism, and abundant consumption. Each and every one of them needs to be reworked to come to terms with the galloping Anthropocene. Granted, such work is difficult, compelling most of us (including me) to rethink old ideals from the ground up. I myself have merely begun to scratch the surface of these issues. But support of a singular equation between capitalism and rapid climate change may tend to insinuate that the other nineteenth- and twentieth-century ideals are okay as they stand.

Sixth, while geologists who coined and used the term "Anthropocene" have themselves often been too generic in their discussions of our responsibility for its production, they have also begun to introduce humanists, human scientists, and activist citizens to a series of geological processes that intersect with different versions of capitalism and other civilizations. Those in the humanities and human sciences—often allergic to such sciences because of the reductionism they have so often encountered in them in the past—must now establish close contact with burgeoning work in the earth sciences, as we help them to refine their thinking about the imbrications between volatile planetary forces and turbulent social processes. Capitalism, in each of its distinctive modes, has become a major geological force; it is also closely entangled with dynamic planetary trajectories with powers of their own.

Those are several reasons that make me hesitate to adopt the term "Capitalocene." That being said, I learn from those who organize their thinking around that idea, and I very much welcome coalitions and alliances forged across these differences. During the contemporary era there is no single center, class, or intellectual hegemony around which resistance and critical coalitions must be formed. More of us must become critical, cross-regional eco-pluralizers today.

The Anthropocene as Planetary Machine

Climate—as an abstract machine periodically shifting and morphing in its dominant components, speed, and trajectories—is imbricated with a host of planetary and cosmic forces. The example of Rome helps to teach that lesson. We can think of the cyclical intensities of sunspot formation, the elliptical pattern of the earth's rotation, the wobble of the earth, and the periodic shift in its tilt. Call these cyclical forcings. There are also intermittent asteroid showers, changes in the ratio of oxygen to carbon and nitrogen, volcanic eruptions, earthquakes, hurricanes, wildfires, and tsunamis. These form less cyclical and more unpredictable forces of volatility. Call them noncyclical drivers. Any conjunction between a forcing and a major driver can induce dramatic climate effects, as the self-organizing history of ice ages, interglacial periods, mass extinction events, desertification, and sharp turns in species evolution shows—and as the rapid organization of the Late Antique Little Ice Age shows again.

The ocean conveyor system, for instance, was formed millions of years ago, well after the oceans had been formed and before any humans appeared to think of themselves as potential masters of the earth. The conveyor carries warm surface water from the Gulf of Mexico north toward Greenland, where cooling, more saline water dives down in a spinning fashion to flow south along the ocean floor until it reaches the Indian Ocean. There the heating water rises again to the surface to flow north toward the Gulf. It is a self-organizing system formed originally out of dissonant connections between climate, wind currents, gravity, the Coriolis effect, and shifting water densities. It also closed down 12,700 years ago when a new ice age formed and somehow stopped the flow. Exactly how it did so remains uncertain, but that the stoppage occurred is known. The effects of the conveyor upon climate on the eastern seaboard of North America and western Europe are dramatic, as they would be in a different way if it collapsed again. The Gulf Stream is now at its weakest level in 1,600 years.[22]

The vicissitudes of the ocean conveyor provide merely one manifestation of how differences in latitude create a highly imperfect index of climate differentials. The first European invaders of Jamestown and Saint Augustine in North America encountered huge problems because the invaders had anchored seasonal estimates of temperature and precipitation on an assumed parallel between latitude and climate. In fact, perhaps partly due to a slowing of the ocean conveyor, the late sixteenth- and early seventeenth-century European invaders encountered a Little Ice Age, a phenomenon that magnified the difference between climate and latitude.[23] Their struggles were bound up with that mistake, as the places they so ruthlessly invaded were much colder and more inhospitable to their traditions of food production than they anticipated.

Let's narrow the focus a bit to explore contemporary intersections between less cyclical, nonhuman amplifiers and the triggers of extractive capitalism to explore the shape and trajectory of the Anthropocene today as an abstract machine. Extractive modes of capitalism, organized around an imperative of growth they are challenged to sustain, pull key triggers. Massive CO_2 emissions, agri-methane releases, and deforestation projects trigger climate warming today, as they did for a couple of centuries before the great acceleration in the 1950s. So extractive capitalism—as well as the dominant modes of consumption and democratic constituencies that press it to sustain its classical course—are key agents in a planetary time machine that exceeds it. But climate, glacier, drought, and acidification effects will not soon diminish to a parallel degree if or when such states simply reverse those triggers and retune the shape and trajectories of their political economies. The assumption of temporal parallelism rests upon ignoring multiple planetary amplifiers set off by the triggers, as well as accelerators set off by intersections between amplifiers. It is as though the classical Newtonian concept of reversible time is being applied in some quarters to processes that exhibit interfolded becomings which do not return to their previous states. Though planetary temporalities can change direction, the reversibility of time is an old Newtonian fairy tale: it is easier to break an egg than to recompose it into a new chick.

If the old capitalist states had taken emergency actions by the middle or late 1980s, the lack of parallel between the force of capitalist emission triggers and temperature rises, glacier melts, drought expansion, ocean acidification, monsoons, and so on would not have not been so severe. Some amplifiers would not have been kicked into gear and others could have been slowed. But that did not happen. In the U.S., to take a key instance, the evangelical/neoliberal resonance machine, as we have already glimpsed, emerged rather rapidly to form the cutting edge of official climate denial and deferral for forty years, showing again how spiritual forces often play roles of importance in larger machines, as they did earlier both in Rome and in the consolidation of northern European industrial capitalism a few centuries ago.

So we must add amplifiers to the list of triggers, cyclical forcings, and noncyclical drivers. An amplifier is a self-augmenting process set in motion by a cyclical forcing, noncyclical driver, or civilizational trigger; the effect of the amplifier intensifies the effects of the others taken alone. Several amplifiers and triggers can, for instance, enter into cascading processes in which each speeds up the pace and/or volume of the others.[24] Here are several noncyclical amplifiers induced by capitalist and noncapitalist emission triggers during this planetary period:

Melted ice absorbs much more solar heat than solid ice, placing the glacier melt rate in a self-promoting spiral.

More rapid iceberg calving in Greenland from heating foments ground vibrations as icebergs rumble down the fjords, spurring shallow earthquakes that place the Helheim Glacier flow in a self-propelling spiral.

Rivers formed on top of melting glaciers dive through cracks and gaps (moulins) in the ice to create flotillas upon which the glacier now floats more rapidly.

Freezing water in the moulins following summer melts exploded the Antarctic Larsen B Ice Shelf in three days in 2002, when glaciologists had previously thought it might take seventy years or more.

As oceans absorb larger amounts of CO_2 and become more highly acidified, their CO_2 absorptive capacity declines and coral reefs are destroyed, further depleting sea life in and around the reefs, depleting food supplies, decreasing CO_2-absorbing plankton, and accelerating the warming spiral.

As the rapid warming of oceans contributes to their rise (along with glacier melts) through higher temperatures that expand the water, the damage to coral reefs combines with the retreat of fish from the warm, tropical waters to colder waters; the stress on tropical and subtropical food supplies will promote migrations and territorial conflicts.

The breakup of the West Antarctic Ice Sheet—the most recent iceberg was the size of Delaware—eliminates previous bulwarks against accelerated movement of the continental glacier.

The heating of oceans and tundra from accumulated CO_2 emissions could release frozen methane clathrates in the tundra and ocean crystals, further accelerating warming (as may have happened during the great extinction event 250 million years ago after eruptions of the Siberian flats).

As the Greenland glacier melt accelerates, enlarged pools of water allow algae to cover more of its surface, reducing the albedo effect (reflection rate of sun rays) from 90 percent to under 20 percent, thus further speeding the pace of the glacier melt.

More open water in the Arctic creates large waves that batter ice on the shores to increase the volume of melted water.

Melting glaciers in Greenland could disrupt or stop the key downward thrust of the ocean conveyor system at its most vulnerable point near Greenland, as the melts pour fresh water onto the ocean surface lighter than the salty water.

The expansion of drought in sub-Saharan Africa and the African Horn press suffering grazers and farmers to cut down more vegetation or flee, decreasing further the CO_2-absorptive capacities of the land, promoting civil wars, increasing refugee pressure, and fostering fascist temptations in the receiving regimes.

Climate warming increases water temperatures in the Gulf Stream and reduces the average speed of Gulf trade winds that propel the increasingly high rotational speed of hurricanes, so that hurricanes become both more intense and remain longer over one zone to dump larger volumes of water upon populated regions.

Intensification of periodic El Niños through climate warming in the Pacific could interrupt monsoon seasons over India and China, placing huge populations at risk; these results, which have occurred before, could in turn unleash a series of volatile political events, including mass starvation, social violence, and swelling refugee drives.

Growing deforestation in Brazil, Columbia, the Gulf states, Congo, and elsewhere—due variously to the needs of subsistence farmers, capital timber projects, and the effects of increasingly intense hurricanes—generate more CO_2 emissions, increasing the rate of forest fires and climate change as they do; the resulting expansion of drought zones again presses many subsistence farmers to clear new forest areas.

That is a short list of self-organizing amplifiers as planetary temporalities. They bump and fold into each other as they form an abstract machine with several cultural spiritualities and capitalist triggers already noted. They accentuate pressure on capitalist states to change their ways, or to fend off growing refugee pressures, build territorial walls, and forge fascist responses to an accelerating planetary machine.

The machine itself is forged by movements back and forth between the entrenched priorities of extractive capitalism, the growing lead times between drilling and production in a world where oil drilling and fracking require more extreme technologies, white ressentiment against other regions and peoples of color, neoliberal hubris, race and class exploitation, imperial drives, hungry dispossessed peoples, impositions of selective austerity, growing fossil fuel emissions, agricultural deforestation, refugee pressures, sea-level rise, spiraling glacier melts, expanding drought zones, changes in the ocean conveyor, loss of fisheries, and ocean acidification. In this convoluted system of multitemporalities on the move, disparate forces and agencies work within and upon each other to produce a planetary machine in which no single factor, agency, or force is entirely in charge—an abstract, planetary machine, with a momentum of its own.

To curtail this machine will take radical action spurred by loosely coordinated minorities of diverse faiths and social positions located in several regions—including protesting minorities in old capitalist states and activist minorities in regions that now incur the most severe suffering from the machine.

The roaring climate machine cannot simply be reversed or halted at this time: the interacting triggers and amplifiers in motion mean that even a radical reduction in atmospheric emissions (triggers) would not be matched immediately by a parallel reduction in warming, drought expansion, rising seas, extreme storms, forest fires, species losses, hurricane severity, civil wars, refugee migrations, and ocean acidification.

Sure, a surprising event could possibly break the right way at the right moment, as new political pressures build in several regimes to change power grids, reconstitute wasteful infrastructures of consumption, and rework the cultural ethos of desire and consumption.[25] Or an unexpected fuel invention could rapidly displace demands for gasoline-powered vehicles and fossil-powered electric companies in several countries. Or a massive new volcanic eruption could cool the atmosphere for a few years, giving people time to reduce harmful emissions and rework their political economies. However, the last option would be a mixed blessing at best, as it would kill thousands of people in its vicinity, threaten monsoons, interfere with crop yields in several regions, confine air travel in others, and foster rapid warming again after the heavier dust particles fell to earth and the carbon releases remained in the atmosphere.

More likely, a crazy scheme of cloud seeding, or something like it, will gain corporate and state enthusiasm as regimes become desperate, even if the scheme threatens the monsoons that nourish billions of people outside of the temperate zones and unleashes other self-organizing developments currently unknown.

As things look now, it is unlikely that concerted action from several regimes will reverse this planetary machine in the short term. But it is possible to slow down its acceleration through an activist assemblage of critical constituencies mobilized across several regions to rework capitalist institutions of investment, production, and consumption, retool the spiritual tone that now occupies so many institutions, and enact mitigation and reparation payments to regions that have contributed the least and suffer the most from this galloping planetary machine.[26] The key is to put internal and external pressure on pivotal states, corporations, churches, universities, localities, banks, and unions at the same time. Such efforts will be difficult to mobilize and sustain, but there is nothing in the very logic of capitalist society that makes it impossible to pursue them. And the stakes are high.

If and as these modes of cross-regional activism gain traction, critical thinkers also need to rework creatively a series of contending nineteenth-century ideals of material abundance and spiritual hubris that no longer cohere with the future possibilities we can anticipate in such a rocky world. For if several existing regimes incite more and more disbelief, cynicism, resignation, ressentiment, and nihilism—depending upon the constituency involved—critics of the status quo must also concede that the most familiar counterideals do not excite that much confidence either. Fascism can readily fill the vacuum if, when democratic capitalism founders, other familiar alternative ideals have lost their luster, too. They, too, require reconstitution during an era of capitalist hegemony, asymmetries of regional suffering, the multiplication of planetary amplifiers, and an accelerating climate machine.

I hope to join others in pursuing that task in a future study.

Three

The Lure of Truth

When I went up to Cambridge early in the 1880s . . . nearly everything was supposed to be known about physics. . . . By the middle of the 1890s there were a few tremors . . . but no one sensed what was coming. By 1900 the Newtonian physics were demolished. . . . Still speaking personally, it had a profound effect on me. I have been fooled once [by the claim of certainty] and I am damned if I will be fooled again. . . . There is no more reason to think that Einstein's relativity is final than Newton's *Principia*. The danger is dogmatic thought."

—ALFRED NORTH WHITEHEAD, *Dialogues of Alfred North Whitehead*

———

I like the word ["curiosity"]; it evokes the care one takes of what exists and might exist; a sharpened sense of reality . . . ; a readiness to find what surrounds us strange and odd . . . ; a lack of respect for the traditional hierarchies of what is important and fundamental.

—MICHEL FOUCAULT, "The Masked Philosopher"

The correspondence model of truth has fallen on hard times, partly because it encourages the contestable assumption that the world presents a highly legible face to us and partly because more analysts have come to appreciate how the diverse historical shapes assumed by varying subjects of truth persistently infiltrate what counts as true. The cultural diversity of tendencies to engage the world and the species limits to human subjectivity meet the possibility that the ways of the world may exceed our capacities of knowledge and technologies of experiment. The return of the view that nonhuman modes of subjective striving both inhabit and exceed us makes things more, not less, complex, since these conjunctions open the door to bursts of real creativity in the world. One probable key to the persistence of the subject/object dichotomy in Euro-American philosophy and the social sciences was its promise to make the issue of truth more manageable. But those days are gone. The noise, litter, scars, resistances, and anomalies we repeatedly encounter—while their sites vary across time and place—may form part of experience as such. And, certainly, humans generate considerable noise and litter for nonhuman subjectivities.[1]

Coherence and pragmatic theories show promise, particularly in the ways they link the pursuit of truth to practical problems. But do they emphasize enough how cultivation of new modes of responsiveness to the world poses questions of existential tolerability to the responsive agents? Are they too riddled with a certain existential complacency? Neo-Nietzscheans, such as Foucault in his middle phase, trouble several of these notions. They do so by exposing fugitive noises, surpluses, and resistances that historical regimes of truth encounter. But do these admirable interventions themselves not exhibit an aspiration to truth? It appears that the later Foucault would answer yes to this question. It appears that he pursued a positive image of truth to both combat classic images and open subjects to enhanced experimentalism. He soon addressed the question of "the courage of truth," particularly in cultural settings where it was dangerous to speak truth. The paradox of truth marks a certain mismatch between a desire for truth disentangled from variabilities of human subjectivity and the sense that the shape of these latter variations must be included in the calculus.

The constructive task is to come to terms with the lure of truth without rendering truth too simple in doing so. If an image of truth is one-dimensional, it can surely be invoked every day to show how others do not live up to it. But it does not provide much of a positive guide for the pursuit of knowledge. The more simple a model of truth, the more its purveyors are tempted to spend their lives proving only how others fail to meet it. That is one of the attractions of pure negativity. And yet in an age of fake news it is important to save truth.[2] In an age of fake news, we must also resist internal and external pressures to force the pursuit of truth into molds set by the great simplifiers. We thus attempt a high-wire walk, replete with jesters and tarantulas ready to throw the walkers off balance.

To appreciate the complexity of the quest and to hazard responses along the way, consider an imaginary dialogue between Michel Foucault starting in his middle phase and Alfred North Whitehead. Each thinker articulates his views in the early going. Then the dialogue assumes its own course, as each absorbs some points from the other as the dialogue proceeds. That is why the two personae are called F and W.

F   Truth is a thing of this world. Once a regime of truth hardens into, say, accepted truths about biological evolution, the order of capitalism, the human capacity to tame nature, the necessary shape of the human subject, and the norms of gender duality, critical encounters may soon disclose how a complex historical regime of perception, normality, and ontological hope is invested in the products that emerge. Call that genealogy.

Consider the case of Herculine Barbin, set in the nineteenth century.[3] Was this anomalous being a woman? A man? A mistake of nature? Well, she was raised in a convent as a girl. But h/er bodily composition, social designations, modes of desire, and sense of self did not mesh well with the cultural norms of either male or female. The nineteenth-century scientists, priests, judges, doctors, and journalists who studied Alex/ina insistently imposed a set of binary norms upon h/er body. Alexina lacked this male trait; she exceeded that female one. H/er desires were anomalous to some, wicked to others. The will to truth, set in the binary categories of gender, injured and defeated Alex/ina until the anomalous being committed suicide.

That same gender binary reassured others that some biocultural traits dominant in them corresponded to the dictates of nature as such, though it doubtless filled many with secret anxieties about whether their hormonal secretions and bodily dispositions sufficiently corresponded to the culturally ingrained bio-norm. Better to let Alex/ina die by suicide than to allow such an anomalous life to challenge the norm of gender duality invested in the overlapping regimes of science, faith, habit, ritual, language, law, and gender anxiety. Do we truly need a true sex?

W You present a powerful example, one that compels us to rethink the tacit sense that the basic rules of Western grammar are well equipped to designate the world, or even (as Kant would insist) to represent it as it must be for us. The subject/predicate form of Indo-European sentences may misread the way of the world. That form tends to focus on objects as settled things and to underplay their temporal entanglements in a processual world. It also exaggerates the primordial unity of the subject. I concur that when you look into things more deeply—when you explore the history of imbrications between European sciences, juridical processes, theologies, unconscious cultural norms, and established scientific testing instruments—the suspicion grows that a regime of insidious disciplines is often brought to bear to help to make the world conform to the categories brought to it. The issues involved do not merely speak to how the world is represented—though they do involve that—but also to how dominant technologies and spiritualities of the day work to shape it to fit their demands. The facts of gender duality become crystallized within a complex background of assumptions, technologies, disciplines, and theories.[4] Authorities, for instance, could impose surgery upon Alexina to make h/er body move closer to the cultural norm of gender duality.

You address how historically shaped subjectivities help to engender the correspondences they observe and how those who deviate from these norms are often said to lack something essential. The dominant subjectivities and technologies, then, help to constitute a regime of truth that helps to model objects it purports to represent.

Of course, nothing in what you say requires us always to be skeptical about every claim supported by evidence from diverse sources. Thus the historical record provides ample evidence that the United States invaded Iraq in 2002 rather than the other way around. At a higher level of complexity, we now have several types of evidence (historical narratives, agricultural records, ice cores, tree rings, isotopes, records of drought expansion, pollen deposits, the collapse of the Mayan Empire, etc.) that the Medieval Warming Period was hotter in Europe and the Americas than the immediately preceding and following eras were.

Still, your own example of how multiple pressures enact gender duality suggests that often a disciplinary regime helps to foster or impose the very phenomenon it purports merely to represent. Your example counsels us to work again upon received languages of expression and designation, as well as on the biocultural organization of specific regimes of perception and bodily practice. It incites us to participate in more lived experiments as we test the established limits of what is natural or necessary. It may encourage us to explore more profoundly how, as Nietzsche would say, "the remains of an old theology" roam around in the premonitions, disciplines, and languages of secular judgment that inhabit us.[5]

By "remains" I mean not merely old categories and explicit assumptions in this or that domain—though they too are important—but also loose ends and vague attractions that may persist after refined belief in a relevant doctrine has lapsed. Residues left behind after a shift in overt belief may continue to work upon us on a visceral level. I sometimes call these the scars of the past. Consider how, in *The Eternal Sunshine of the Spotless Mind*, Kirsten Dunst, playing a minor character, finds herself vaguely attracted to the director of the Memory Erasure Institute. Her recollection of their earlier affair has been erased by memory technicians. But each recollection subsists in a dense network of layered memories, so that remnants of the erased recollections can now assume the form of vague, intense attractions, something like the way a middle-aged man may stare unconsciously at a woman who looks strangely like his mother when she was young, or the way the mind wanders when the default system of action-oriented perception is relaxed to allow unconscious memories and events to ramble around more freely.

What if, however, both the recollections and the remains (or scars) attached to them had been erased by those technicians? Well, the preliminary orientations needed to perceive, think, and act would have been expunged from the Dunst character too. She would have become a carrier of the spotless mind the recollection erasure crew had tried so hard to avoid producing. The crew only wanted to erase a specific set of recollections while retaining several other recollections, memory-soaked dispositions, and remains entangled with them. The very difficulties they faced show again how memories are both entangled and layered. Some dimensions of memory exceed recollection: each dimension helps to infuse the composition of experience. Nothing in the world is purely epiphenomenal. Everything carries some degree of efficacy.

Without remains and loose ends, thinking, feeling, and searching themselves would flatten out. With them the adventure of thought periodically encounters turning points that may feel initially like gropings in the dark.

In the nineteenth-century world of Alex/ina, numerous ritual enactments and embedded norms of the day—think of en-gendered habits of walking, dress, voice, facial demeanor, enacted presumptions of gender authority, gendered grammar, differential ethical injunctions, and so on—drew many who disagreed with one another on other counts to assume that en-gendered duality corresponds to natural duality. A set of vague attractions and antipathies bolstered these settled dispositions, expressing the remains of theologies and philosophies that many had begun to question on the more refined registers of belief, as when you drop an old belief in an omnipotent God but continue to assume that morality itself must assume a lawlike form. Rituals of the day become implanted in visceral premonitions of culture, as when an American finds a feeling of disgust rising in him when he sees a chicken stomach floating in the delicious soup of an Asian host even when he believes that such a feeling is ridiculous.

I too took gender duality for granted in my daily life and philosophical work, even though I worked hard to recompose mind/body, nonlife/life, free will/determinism, and theological/secular dualities that remained in force when I was writing in the 1920s and '30s. But don't forget: in exposing how the ritual/disciplinary/linguistic formation of gender duality is set in a larger regime of truth through the potent example of Alex/ina, you remain drawn to the lure of truth.

Don't you think, for instance, that quantum theory—after upending classical models that had more or less reduced the world to simple atoms and efficient modes of causality—constituted a major advance in science? Is it not closer to the truth than the theories that preceded it? I must say, too, that new theories in evolutionary biology of horizontal gene transfer move them closer than neo-Darwinism to my own process philosophy of a world replete with many sites of creative agency—closer to that philosophy, indeed, than to either Darwinism or neo-Darwinism.[6]

Is it not, similarly, closer to the truth to attend to a plurality of gender potentialities—to be culturally elaborated in open ways through lived experiments of social life—than to stick with the cruelties of the old duality? What positive image of truth do you support after showing us how power is invested in the norms of gender duality and the subjectivities through which they are sustained in a regime of truth?

F   I am pleased that you discern tensions between layered, socially contoured subjectivities and a correspondence model of truth. The model of correspondence situates the idea of representing fixed states at the apex of thought. But many processes—eggs, stem cells, bacteria, brains, viruses, climate, species, solar systems—go through robust periods of metamorphosis. I also appreciate your reputation as the philosopher who both decomposed a series of entrenched metaphysical dualities and pressed us to come to terms with the uncanny logic of real creativity in a processual world composed of multiple tiers of becoming moving at different speeds and modes of complexity. There are periods of relative stability in most domains, but we concur that situations of morphing and real uncertainty are more common than previously thought. It is important to apply techniques of the self to ourselves not only for ethical reasons but for ontological reasons too. Open philosophies of time and correspondence philosophies of truth have long been at war with one another, as I explored in *The Order of Things*.

Certainly a new theory may resolve some problems in an old one. But I do doubt that such changes assume a linear pattern of advance. Scientists might think they are riding a train of linear progress and then encounter a shock that throws things up for grabs. Maybe inquiry after that shock takes a sharp turn, irreducible to the project of linear progressive images of science. Maybe another turn in an unforeseen direction is taken later. The new biologies of epigenesis and horizontal gene transfer make us look again at some themes in

Lamarck, for instance, after he had long been left for dead by neo-Darwinians. Symbiogenesis, whereby horizontal evolution occurs, challenges neo-Darwinism to the core; if it turns out to be widespread, it translates the old oak tree of species evolution into a tangled web or even a rhizome.

A science periodically gropes in the dark and sometimes is compelled to look back at old regimes it had previously left behind. Take, on a different plane, how a devastating European holocaust pressed many who had believed in powerful trends toward civilizational progress to reexamine threads in Sophocles that previously had been consigned to peculiar Greek orientations to fate.

Let me dramatize—emphasize to bring out—one possible difference between us, a difference that pulls me closer, say, to Sophocles than to Hegel. I sense that you believe that the multifaceted world of becoming is more attuned in principle to refined human capacities of knowledge and belonging than I suspect them to be. I even suspect that you insistently project that the world must be well disposed to us to deserve human responsiveness. Such underground "musts" are existential and not merely logical. Think of phrases such as "the world must be governed by a god" or "it must assume the shape of linear progress." Existential musts often inhabit phrases said by those who enunciate them to embody only logical musts.

Let me put it this way: you remain attracted to romantic images that helped to inspire your valuable critiques of binary logics in science and philosophy in something like the way the magnetic signatures of sea turtles—exquisitely attuned to the earth's magnetic field—draw breeding turtles back toward their early nesting grounds from thousands of miles away.[7] Note, however, how they adjust their final course if the old nesting grounds have become overgrown by human settlements.

The subtle power of remains, loose ends, and lures. For I agree with you that subtle pulls on experience include and exceed the rather clumsy organization of the five senses; vague lures penetrate visceral dimensions of being. Even the tacit experience of human orientation in the world exceeds the multimodal organization of the five senses. You would appreciate the recent discovery of mirror neurons in neuroscience as well as that of olfactory sensors in human beings that promote visceral intercommunications between organs below conscious awareness of the individual. Let alone new work on intercommunications between the gut and the brain. These microsubjectivities help give vibrancy to the affective tone of experience. There is more to experience than perception through the five senses; even those senses must become highly disciplined before they can be synthesized together. Bacteria in the biome, with ministrivings of their own, help to compose our moods, as you already surmised presciently in 1927.

You have also been brilliant in decomposing Eurocentric transcendental arguments—the mode of definitive argumentation that purported, first, to identify the defining qualities of the human subject as such and, second, to establish how such subjects must represent a world of objects. That is why you insert the probable ineliminability of speculation into the very fabric of philosophical inquiry. I concur. I also insist that wherever speculation operates, contestability is apt to hover around it. The element of contestability arrives in part because of divergent lures pulling upon different constituencies at such critical junctures.

So let me be clear about one aspect of my—as you would call it—speculative view about human relations to several nonhuman processes. There is no reliable prediscursive providence disposing bumpy planetary processes of diverse sorts strongly in our favor. Several are not reliably predisposed to our welfare.[8] The sense that they must be expresses the remains of an old theology of an omnipotent God and progressive history once dominating Europe. Remains. That is one reason, again, I think techniques of the self are so important both to the reconstruction of an old ontology and to the quality of ethical life. These are techniques—such as priming your dreams before bedtime, meditating, neurotherapy, going for a run after stumbling over a problem—that reach into embedded dispositions and remain below the level of conscious scrutiny. I concur with you that the searchlight of consciousness into the interior of the self is weak.

Human subjectivities, varying significantly across time and place, are formed through atmospheric infusions, dense social routines, institutional demands, and social disciplines; we then carry them to a world we both represent and strive to organize to fit more closely the representations. Moreover, the modes through which the world is organized recoil back into the organization of the human sensorium. We are not entirely reducible to such cultural disciplines, however, since they themselves can endow us with creative capacities. I am not a reductionist. Nonetheless, the weight of historically organized disciplines does flow into specific tendencies. Soon resistances, surprises, illegibilities, and noises are apt to be encountered, as you engage the tensions between an unfolding world and the organizational powers of this or that disciplinary regime.

I take the recurrence of such loose ends and noise to suggest that the world is not reliably predisposed to human aspirations and interests, though I acknowledge they could be interpreted (speculatively) otherwise. Often, those who suffer most under an existing regime of truth take the lead in pushing against its hegemony in the domains of gender, sexuality, state religious injunctions, scientific soundness, and secular discipline. The onto-epistemic struggles that ensue also involve political struggles against a dominant power/knowledge regime, the insurrection of subjugated knowledges.

Critics might revise dominant theories to respond to these resistances, often doing so today by trying to adjust them to the larger demands of extractive capitalism. And once again new resistances and anomalies are encountered. Do you think we can hope to devise a theory in which all anomalies and volatile remainders disappear? Is that the lure pulling you? Do you also think the nonhuman world is predisposed to us in its own modes of organization? What do you imagine dinosaurs or Neanderthals thought about that question during their respective heydays? If the earth is so disposed to human beings in particular, is this because of a providential God? A set of lucky coincidences? The secular tendency of multiple trajectories to harmonize over time? How do you square your distinctive appreciation of real creativity in the world to these other existential assumptions? Does a mosquito express a similar presumption when it lands on your warm, juicy skin just before you slap it?

W First a confession. I suppose I have been attracted tacitly to the idea that nonhuman temporal trajectories are somewhat more predisposed to us during this cosmic epoch than you find yourself to be, partly because of my aristocratic experience and partly because I am acutely aware of the impressive logics and instruments the sciences have devised over the last few centuries to subject previous conclusions and current guesses to tests of consistency and observation. But I also contend—as you see—that speculative elements are involved in forging an intercoded philosophy of subjectivity, truth, science, creativity, and time. It is just that the edges of speculation themselves shift over time, and we have reason to hope that newly formed edges register creative advances over the old ones.

I am also impressed with evidence of how elements in the world that once stood in an antagonistic relation to each other sometimes resonate back and forth until those differences become harmonized into a more complex set of contrasts in the same entity. The formation of the nucleated bacterium from the ingression of loose DNA into a non-nucleated cell may fit such a model. Some invaded bacteria might perish. But, eventually, a creative adaptation to such ingressions is organized, generating a nucleated cell where none had existed in the biosphere before: creative harmonization creates room for a more complex entity than heretofore. The very emergence of organic evolution itself arose from this incredible process of harmonization. Examples can be found in human cultures too, whereby, say, an unruly form of capitalism adapted itself to new exigencies through political struggles that spawned social democracy.

My major concern about your work, however, is how hesitant you were to appreciate robustly the multiplicity and variety of intersecting subjectivities in this world. The world itself is composed of a wide plurality of subjects, according to my evidence-based speculations, including bacteria, bees, fungi, leopards, olfactory sensors, and human hormonal secretions. So the powers of subjectivity are not confined to human cultures alone. Indeed, we would not be subjects ourselves, unless we were also populated by a series of intersecting microsubjects.

Your flirtations with human exceptionalism distress me. Animal and plant strivings, bacterial and viral agencies, lava flows and electron synchronicities: they all convey differing degrees and modes of agency on the way. Intersections between them also help to compose the temporal course of the world, as when the ingression of spirochete bacteria into the neuronal tissue of a human embryo may have helped to improve the future suppleness of human thinking.[9] A horizontal mode of evolution.

Again, the human self involves complex coordination of both multiple subjectivities inside it and the receipt of diverse forces or ingressions from outside.[10] I am impressed by new work in neuroscience that appeared after my speculations on this topic.[11] This means that when I advance a coherence model of truth, the quest for coherence addresses relations between multiple, heterogeneous, shifting subjectivities. I do not accept the Cartesian subject/object duality, the very duality joined to human exceptionalism that set the background from which several theories of truth were defined during the world hegemony of Euro-America.

The more aware we become of a multitude of microagencies—such as microbes, neuronal infusions, hormonal flows, and communicating rhythms and vibrations across milieux—that help to compose our moods, prejudgments, and thinking, the more we sense human subjectivity to be a biosocially organized multiplicity on the move. Awareness of this complexity does not reduce us to blind effects of other determinations, as many neo-Kantians seem to fear; for the free will/determinist debate is precisely one of the binary simplicities I supplant. Rather, complex exchanges between multiple subjectivities complicate the tonalities and expressions of human subjectivity, creativity, and the quest for truth. I thus replace the flat objects that have populated many philosophies since Descartes with a multitude of subjectivities of different sorts helping to define through rhythmic exchanges what the world becomes. Recast the subject/object dichotomy. It is insufficient merely to criticize the subject/object dichotomy. It must be recast.

To grasp how creativity works through and across encultured selves and assemblages—though it is impossible to provide a sufficient explanation of the process when the assumption of real creativity is embraced—let me focus more closely on how scars of the past work.[12] These scars (or remains in the Nietzschean vocabulary with which you are familiar) operate in microorganisms in some ways and humans in others. Let's focus on the latter now.

You may reach a crossroad and find yourself—after a moment of hesitation in which several unconscious microprocesses reverberate back and forth—turning down one fork rather than another. The fork not taken does not disappear. It persists as a festering node of unconsolidated pluripotentialities. You can call this the past that never was, if you want to speak in paradoxical terms.

When an unexpected situation is encountered later, that nest of pluripotentialities may be aroused again. A vague attraction between the new event and the fork not taken now arises. The resonances back and forth between the past that never was and the new situation could, doubtless, result in an impasse or collapse. But sometimes such resonances issue in something new. The new entity might be an evolutionary change, an idea, a strategy, a novel political temper, or a new religious devotion. The creative element in this process cannot be simply reduced either to a prior intention or to chance. It involves dissonant reverberations between scars of the past, a new situation, and—in the case of humans at least—the bubbling up of a new possibility into consciousness for further reflection. The task now is to forge images of subjectivity, world, and truth that do not arbitrarily foreclose attention to such processes of creativity.

Now in your early studies of entanglements between power, subjectivity, and social discipline within a regime of truth, you at first tended to construe the modern human subject as a being that struggles to impose its agenda upon the world, to constitute a world. And, impressively, you showed repeatedly how such attempts at constitution often encounter modes of resistance, anomaly, uncertainty, suffering, and so on. The ethico-political task, at that point, is to amplify resistances to such subjugations.

You often focused on disciplines and violences that were preaccomplished, in the sense that disciplinary norms of the day treated them either as results to which people had already implicitly consented or violences necessary to the advance of civilization as such. Alexina provides a case in point. But the instances proliferate. Locke, for example, acted as if people had implicitly consented to private property in the state of nature; Kant acted as if a killer had consented to capital punishment through the act of murder; Tocqueville acted as if Amerindians necessarily faced near extinction because their understandings of gods and nature placed them on a low rung of the historic ladder of progress; Hegel acted as if the pursuit of a world of sovereign states carried with it implicit acceptance of hegemony by a world historical state; the market automatism celebrated by classical liberals and neoliberals was said to show how necessary colonial exploitation and internal inequality are to rational, capitalist growth.

Reformers who try to relieve the latter injuries are told constantly by neoliberals that their good intentions must inevitably backfire. As neoliberalism slides perilously close to fascism today in several states, the neoliberal dismissal of the liberal do-gooder has morphed into neofascist assaults on the snowflake: the liberal or radical who both cares too much about others and melts when pressed hard by white nationalists and militarists. The shift in this terminology of criticism reveals the slide of neoliberalism itself from the world of dog whistles to a regime of foghorns.

The above list of truths in Locke and company was said to be implied by what was known within what you call a regime of truth. A genealogy, as I learn from you, roughs up such a network of assumptions, expectations, impositions, disciplines, and demands; it opens the door to new rounds of critical politics. Indispensable! Especially if it is also extended to the understandings of nature and time projected by Locke, Kant, Tocqueville, Hegel, and neoliberalism.

In your later work, however, the language of discipline and imposition becomes more overtly ambiguated. You explore how human subjects can become more responsive to the effects on others of hegemonic priorities, disciplines, and assumptions, how they can work on themselves to amplify generous strains already circulating quietly in them as well as to appreciate some complexities of the world disowned by established regimes of truth.[13] The constituted and constitutive subject now begins to fester, under pressure of tactics to foster exploratory, responsive, courageous subjects—not merely through a refined logic of reflexivity but also through arts of the self and a dissident politics that rouses subjugated knowledges.

Arts or techniques of the self, for instance, express your own awareness that since the internal spotlight of consciousness is weak—and I very much agree with you on that theme—critical reflexivity, which aims at first making a desire more transparent and then revising it through new bouts of thinking, is insufficient to reform default modes of habit, perception, and judgment. A politics that emphasizes the arousal of subjugated knowledges (as you do) thus carries with it the understanding that democratic representation through elections—while important—needs to be counterbalanced by social movements to press new rights and identities into the world. The latter provide the vehicles, you could say, by which creativity operates in politics.

Is this not the juncture at which a positive image of truth gestates? An image that negotiates the complexities of disciplinary power, subjectivity, available evidence, and vague lures as it strives to generate coherence between them in response to new events? Yes, such a complex image—because it is composed of multiple elements that can begin to fall out of attunement to each other—constitutes a problematic rather than a systematic philosophy.[14] It is not always clear which adjustments should be made where. Truth now functions as an aspiration or lure rather than being entirely reducible to a unified set of criteria. Any attainment of rough coherence between its constitutive elements becomes entangled with a set of dispositions, assumptions, and speculations, some of which themselves may be called into question again by the shock of a new situation. Truth is now both a thing of this world and a plural set of standards and aspirations to guide life and inquiry. Does not your cultivation of more exploratory, responsive selves pull you in such a direction? And, besides, does not enhanced responsiveness seek to valorize conjunctions between the cultivation of human care for the world and creativity? You evince an attachment to the diversity of life and the world that infiltrates the exploratory searches you undertake.

I suppose the day that the Constantinian creed of a sovereign, omnipotent, personal God faced sharp challenges, the quest for truth as correspondence also became rattled. God, atoms, sense data, the atomic individual, and a national culture have now all now been dislodged from their serial roles as irreducible foundations. Now, for those who take such a turn, truth, subjectivity, power, experimentalism, and attachment to the world can become bound loosely together into a problematic. No? And now any entangled element might be prodded at a key juncture by a new event or analysis in a way that jostles several others. For example, the renewed appreciation of nonhuman subjectivities in Euro-American thought reopens questions about the place and power of transcendental arguments in this domain. Some arguments Kant advanced about the shape appearance must assume to persons as such are now shown to rest upon quaint Eurocentric assumptions.[15] This turn beyond the human exceptionalism of Kant also encourages many to reopen communication with non-Western modes of human/nonhuman perspectivalism (or animism as some call it), a series of outlooks previously relegated to an inferior standing in Euro-American thought. Inferior because participants in those problematics do not accept the dichotomy between living cultures and dead nature we ourselves now increasingly find to be problematic. Truth is both a lure and a thing of this world.

To sharpen the above themes, let me say that at any specific time we participate in one or more regimes of truth composed of multiple elements of the sorts noted, including the vague lures to truth that are experienced as attractors. The latter may be lodged in the loose ends of a regime or the dicey resonances between scars from the past and a new situation. If—as I speculate to be true—there is indeed real creativity in the world, we can also anticipate that no regime of truth will be final. New entities will flow or bump into being. Truth now loses its status as a pure presence beyond the world signified through such words as God or Substance. The lure of truth periodically pulls adventurers beyond the contours of an installed regime.

Since there is—according to this experience-based speculation—no singular end point to a world endowed with elements of real creativity, we may project that such an interplay between regimes and lures never closes down entirely. Or it does not at least as long as agents are capable of pursuing lures of truth. Between regime and lure resides the musicality of the search.

To be more precise, truth is a lure in a double sense: first, in the sense that when a truth is defined within an ongoing regime we feel a pull toward acceptance of it, even if that pull is weakened or drowned by others such as self-interest or existential anxiety; second, in the sense that when an old regime of truth starts to crack or ripple, we may feel more strongly yet the pull of vague remains and attractions that inspire us to forge a new or modified regime.[16]

F   I must say yes to several of your queries and claims. One source of attachment or pull toward the rich fecundity of this world is the persisting intuition many have that we participate modestly, as individuals and assemblages, in larger moments of creativity that exceed us. And that numerous nonhuman processes exceeding civilizational control help to engender new events and encounters. Indeed, read capaciously in relation to the contemporary condition, your work teaches us how existential demands of the Euro-American world are wired into many capitalist practices: the separation of humanity from nature, the insistence of time as linear and progressive, a hubristic image of the mastery of nature, and tendencies to evade the courage of truth whenever events press against those existential desires and demands.

Pragmatic and existential elements must thus be addressed in the aspiration to truth itself, an aspiration to establish coherence between the problems we encounter and the multiple elements composing a regime of truth. An aspiration that pulls upon us as we are drawn to it. Indeed, we must not only pursue truth but cultivate the courage to express it when authorities seek to repress it and to face up to it ourselves when doing so threatens existential demands and hopes obdurately installed within us.[17] The courage of truth points in two directions.

Neither of us is an idealist, in the sense of denying that pressures from the world intrude upon thinking. But our attention to events and problems means that we do not think the intrusions themselves suffice to determine the responses.[18] The idealist/realist debate needs reconfiguration if these speculations about moments of real creativity are to carry weight.

But let me dramatize an issue that has already been posed in this posthumous exchange. You and I became intellectual personae upon our deaths—though it may have taken some a longer time to endow you with that status. Each of us attempted to die nobly, thinking perhaps that love of the richness of life carries with it an obligation to affirm death as one of the conditions of life. During those lives each advanced a series of themes and contentions, accompanied by minor chords circulating through them we did not play up ourselves. To plumb the thought of a philosophical persona in the face of new encounters is often to dramatize aspects of their thought that merely subsisted as seeds of potentiality when they lived.[19] Personae exceed the themes they themselves had themselves emphasized as they are dragged into the future by others.

This strange relation between old personae and new thinking can be accentuated when problems arise that the personae did not themselves address. I speak now as one persona to another during a time in which some things have become apparent that both of us were blind to when we were alive.

So, yes, the cultivation of refined modes of responsiveness is crucial to the pursuit of truth, and presumptive responsiveness is also essential to the positive quality of ethical life. Responsiveness, for you, may have had two edges: first, to a world that exceeds our current categories and is endowed with potential for creativity; second, to a world that is responsive to our needs if and when we become reflectively attuned to it. I now accept the first quest for attunement, but I call into question the emphasis you give to the second expectation, assumption, or hope. Your language of "creative advance" of the universe, of the "advance of civilization," of new "harmonies" creatively forged out of old "antagonisms" to engender new complexity—all these phrases suggest a difference between us on the second register. I am, so to speak, more Nietzschean than you on that issue, even though I too have felt tremors of the romanticism discernible in your work. I see now how my early emphasis on the disciplinary consolidation of subjects may allow you and others to elide the importance of this second difference between us—a point I did not myself sort out so sharply in my early work.

One way to put the difference is that you did recognize the role of tragedy in life—when failure to act wisely during a narrow moment of opportunity locks a tragic outcome into place that could have been otherwise. But you were less drawn than I to what might be called a tragic vision of human/nonhuman possibility in the world. New attunements to the nonhuman world might show several open and intertwined temporal systems with which the human estate is entangled to be less reliably consonant with our needs and interests than you had imagined. I now appreciate more fully how you recast the subject/object dichotomy and how you acknowledge a world composed of multiple intersecting temporalities, even though I do not trace agency into every planetary force.[20] But such amendments could also be interpreted to pose challenges to both the image of a pliable, nonhuman world predisposed to human mastery—a view you nobly contest—and its hitherto favorite debating partner, an organic image of potential harmony between us and the earth. The latter is a view you may be more tempted by.

I speculate it to be true that the world is less predisposed to harmony with us than you may feel it to be. Moreover, such an unruly world is worthy of our attachment, care, and curiosity.[21] It enables us to be, allows attachments and periods of joy, and blesses us with modest bouts of creativity when new challenges arise. As a philosopher who evinces care for the linkages between humanity and the way of the world, the challenge to you, perhaps, is to ascertain to what extent you can cultivate care for such an unruly planet, that is, cultivate sympathetic attunement to multiple planetary processes that are periodically volatile.[22]

Let me put more flesh on those bones, posing an issue that neither of us addressed deeply before we became personae. In the *History of Sexuality*, volume 1, I contended that modern disciplinary societies increasingly place the whole world at risk. I placed the risk of a world thermonuclear war at the forefront of attention. That very danger has escalated again. In addition, we now discern more acutely how extractive capitalist, socialist, and communist societies—unevenly of course—have triggered a series of self-amplifying nonhuman processes such as glacier melts, climate warming, desertification, drought, ocean acidification, rising seas, and more intense El Niños that place humans and other species in several regions at severe and growing risk. This awareness becomes more urgent as we chart how capitalist triggers of CO_2 and methane emissions intersect with several nonhuman amplifiers to spur droughts, refugee pressures, anti-immigration campaigns, famine, civil wars, the construction of territorial walls, drives to sharp regional inequality, violent energy conflicts, and neofascist threats to democracy.

Now, in one way your philosophy of multitemporal processes entangling human and nonhuman societies of diverse types carried us closer to such understandings than any other Western philosophy of its day. Your work contested the themes of human exceptionalism and sociocentrism that infused so many Eurocentric theories. You were ahead of the curve in Euro-American thought. In another way, however, your tacit assumptions about planetary processes that are slow-moving and organically predisposed to us if and when we work to harmonize with them did not alert us sufficiently to regionally distributed dangers the nonhuman world periodically carries back to diverse human cultures and the cultures of other species. These dangers are unevenly distributed, certainly, for it is now obvious that several capitalist states pull the most deadly climate triggers today while several other regions incur the most suffering from volatile conjunctions between capitalist triggers and planetary amplifiers. But it is also more apparent how these planetary volatilities exude degrees of autonomy of their own.

Your philosophy both opened a door to these explorations and underplayed the volatility of planetary processes themselves during this cosmic epoch; neither did you enunciate categories that would alert us to the radical asymmetry between zones of the world that create the most suffering and those that face the most. One way to put it is that you appreciated profoundly how planetary and cosmic processes intersect and contaminate one another. But you—writing when the processes were active below the radar of most but before the great acceleration of climate change in the 1950s—did not sense how the pace of several bumpy planetary temporalities has accelerated and is apt to do so for some time. That changes a lot. Nietzsche came much closer to such premonitions than you did. The element of gradualism in the regime of truth you embraced tears at its center.

I did not address those planetary processes either. I even downplayed the cosmic dimension of philosophy that you, Nietzsche, and Deleuze invoke in different ways. But perhaps my account of regimes of truth opened one door needed to think beyond the categories of sociocentrism and planetary gradualism that have haunted much of Eurocentric social theory. Indeed, if we had met together in, say, 1970 when the great acceleration in CO_2 emissions was well underway behind the backs of capitalist and socialist first worlds, we might together have encouraged modes of awareness and response that remained outside each perspective during its time.

To put it another way, your explorations of fecund intersections between the romantic tradition and the shock of quantum theory at the turn of the twentieth century allowed you to compose fertile notions of ingression, concrescence, occasion, spatialization, and creativity among interwoven temporal processes. These human and nonhuman relationalities called into question the sociocentrism in the human sciences of the day as well as recasting a set of modern binaries—nonlife/life, subject/object, mind/body, free will/determinism, nature/culture—that had heretofore shaped Eurocentric sciences and social sciences. You were one of the pioneering Euro-Americans to reset philosophical speculation at the appropriate level of planetary analysis and a world composed of multiple subjectivities and temporalities.

I salute you for that. I lagged behind. But lingering attachments to the remains of romanticism—remains expressed as vague attractions—may have discouraged you from pondering the intensity of periodic threats to species life on the planetary scales you explored. You were lured to a world predisposed to us when we attend to it.[23] We need to attend to it, but you exaggerate its tendencies to harmonize with us.

Nonetheless, as you have said yourself, lures can change as well as regimes, when new encounters and problems arise. This is the element of wisdom in pragmatic theories of truth. They are not to be identified with some narrow criterion of usefulness within a settled regime of, say, either Keynesian or neoliberal capitalism. They convey vague concerns that can inspire us as we seek to become closely attuned to a volatile world we care about.

I am not saying that you were totally wrong about the predisposition of larger spatiotemporal processes to us, then, for much progress could be made by radical changes in current processes of profit, extraction, production, and exploitation, by sensitivity to the larger world, and by new practices of consumption. I am saying that you sustained a current of thinking that is both salutary in one way and urgently in need of modification in another. I discern more sharply now how we were two ships passing in the night, with each carrying cargo the other needed.

W I might, certainly, claim that you exaggerate the degree to which I was pulled by the lure of romanticism. I could even complicate your notion of romanticism, for romantics such as Mary Shelley and Percy

Shelley deviate from the image you project of them. Mary Shelley even penned a late novel called *The Last Man*—after the deaths of so many she loved—that is more existentialist than romantic in the sense you project of the latter term. And her awareness of planetary volatilities was prescient.[24] I might, moreover, say that had extractive capitalist societies transformed themselves to the degree needed during the great acceleration, a higher degree of harmony between Euro-American cultures, other human cultures, and nonhuman forces would have been in the offing. The human population, for instance, is now growing at about a billion a decade, after it had persisted for several hundred thousand years at several million.

It is important not to make too much of those fecund processes by which previous incompatibilities become harmonies in new, more complex formations. Each new complexity, I already insisted in *Process and Reality*, is also occupied by an element of chaos. The element of chaos or noise may help to open the entity to new modes of evolution when disruptive ingressions occur. Decay can set in too, as I insisted, which means that the creative tendency toward greater complexity can be overturned by events.

I could make some points, then. Nonetheless, I concur that I did not attend enough to the depredations of capitalism, to how its practices unleash vast nonhuman forces with cascading powers of their own, to how a variety of nonhuman planetary agencies both created positive conditions for human life (the bacteria that fill the atmosphere with oxygen) and periodically threaten huge swaths of life with devastation (the five mass species extinctions we now know about). Above all, I did not anticipate how the modern acceleration of shifts in glacier fields, the ocean conveyor, climate, drought zones, wildfires, more intense storms, and ocean acidification could soon pose extreme dangers.

I knew that our best thinking within any regime is apt to become insufficient to the world later. But I tacitly imbibed the assumption of planetary gradualism. I may not have heeded enough how Sophocles's advice to tread softly when the jug is full actually relates to our orientations to both human and nonhuman processes. He was one of my heroes. But I now discern more sharply how he folded the vicissitudes of nonhuman nature into the very center of those cultural dramas (through the activity of the gods) set in the volatile geology of the Mediterranean Sea. I now note the plagues, raging seas, and earthquakes, for instance, that populate those dramas. Today, we face a tough situation. If you look merely at recent public debates about the health effects of smoking, damage to the ozone level, the consequences of rapid climate change, and the turbulent role of markets in modern civilizations, a disturbing pattern is discernible. Those who smoke, or work in industries tied to fossil fuels, or work in finance, or hold working-class jobs in industry, and so on, often hope that claims coming from scientists about the dangers of smoking, the sources of the ozone hole, or the effects of capitalist-induced climate change are false. Neoliberal regimes in turn—as they rapidly concentrate more wealth and income upon those at the top of the system—release surplus funds that right-wing donors and think tanks can deploy to amplify public doubts about the truth of scientific claims in those domains. The result is the proliferation of hired hands to muddy the waters of solid scientific findings, inciting disbelief or cynicism in several constituencies already disposed to have those waters muddied. Such doubts soon become tethered to extreme accusations about the motives of those who advance the critical warnings, prepping entire constituencies to listen to neofascist politicians who are out to defeat scientists and government bureaucracies that do respond to these issues. The recent proliferation of right-wing media outlets exacerbates this emergent machine. You were much more alert to how such processes work than I; they have accelerated in recent decades.[25] To me, at least two complementary sources of evasion are worthy of special note. There are, first, climate deniers and casualists who are either too overwhelmed about the Anthropocene to engage it or find it to be too much at odds with their short-term self-interest to do so. There are, second, those who increasingly see how profound and pressing the planetary issues are but feel too queasy in their guts to assume the arduous political projects of remaking their own cultures. Your hero, Nietzsche, would describe the second constellation as carriers of passive nihilism. We have not yet found adequate ways to prod more of them to cultivate the courage of truth with respect to the Anthropocene. They may increasingly sense how planetary forces work, but remains of previous views lingering in them whisper back, "The world ought not to be this way."[26] There are both religious and secular sources of the latter tendency. So these constituencies become immobilized and silent. Two disparate constituencies converging toward denial or diffidence, sometimes under the pressure of suffering and sometimes under that of greed. This is, of course, particularly true in the United States, the current home of the most bloated capitalist state and the most climate denialism.

The world needs even more climate scientists today who embrace the role of what you call the "specific intellectual," the type of scientist willing to draw on their specific expertise to fend off disinformation regimes as they simultaneously admit the fallibility of scientific work. Indeed, the time calls for a proliferation of specific citizen activists from several regions organizing to put pressure on their states from inside and outside at the same time. It is not an easy task, particularly when you find yourself compelled to contest neoliberal economists and financial elites who insist that markets must be allowed to rumble without intensive regulation, even as states provide massive subsidies to support them. I know you do not blame me—or yourself—for a condition neither of us had addressed, even though it was rumbling along beneath our feet. But I must concur that had we listened to some marginal voices during our own times and had also been able to coalesce in the ways you intimate, a planetary warning system might have been offered earlier to a larger world. And I concur that the examples of Sophocles and Mary Shelley disclose how it may have been possible to have done so earlier in the day. Your efforts late in life to come to terms with the plight of stateless boat people—during a time in the 1980s when dominant states systematically ignored them as they roamed the open seas—was both poignant and prescient about the even more demanding conditions we now face. My own sense is that, even now, significant things can be done to mitigate the worst effects of the Anthropocene. But it will require a politics that is more radical than anything I contemplated before I became a persona. The improbable necessity today is to find ways to infuse positive modes of egalitarian austerity into the institutions and ethos of regimes that have heretofore been constructed around fossil extraction and promises of material abundance. A task now so daunting that it helps us to understand the cultural impulses to climate denialism and casualism that have plagued several capitalist states.[27]

I also think that we need to attend to the bumpy intersections between established regimes of truth, vague lures, and new events as we extend and revise our theories. Scientific finality has not been attained. Nor has the finality of truth, more generally. Let's gather our findings together a bit. It appears that we both are pulled by the lure of truth in the double sense of that phrase already noted. We resist neopositivist and rationalist models of truth set in a putative world of entitled human subjects and natural objects. We also oppose cynical proponents of a post-truth world who seek to manipulate masses for their own narrow agendas. We see that the pursuit of truth, particularly at the cutting edges of thought, involves work on multiple, intercoded fronts—including our subjective constitutions, deeply engrained cultural assumptions, the shape of disciplinary practices, the problems that excite us, available evidence, creative responses by diverse subjectivities, the invention of technologies that allow us to hone our powers of experiment and evidence, and vague attractors that pull us.[28] We cannot reduce truth to a simple set of criteria uninfluenced by vague presuppositions and disciplinary practices, though we do concur that its pursuit invokes coherence tests across multiple processes. We must engage old and new multiplicities that exceed those acknowledged by many earlier Euro-American theorists. We suspect that speculation is apt to continue at the shifting edges of inquiry and that new tests will support some speculations over others. We concur that a new event can pull us back to the drawing board in a surprising way, calling upon us to dig again into this or that aspect of an old theory recently thought to have been left in the dustbin or to forge new concepts that break with old habits. We seek to refine responsive subjectivities to formulate problems more sharply, to respond to a changing world, to support decolonial movements, to respect nonhuman subjectivities that had been displaced by the old subject/object dichotomy, and to reduce the face of opacity the world presents to us with respect to problems we now discern. Our shared legacy today, perhaps, is to mine the tension between historical regimes of truth organized almost behind the backs of investigators and vague lures to truth that can be drawn upon to experiment with revisions in a regime. To invoke merely one example, neither of us would accept the analytic/synthetic dichotomy advanced by logical empiricists in the postwar period—that dichotomy provided one of the keys to the regime of truth so many accepted. The collection of data within the compass of that demand must be attacked through philosophical inquiry that attends to the loose ends slipping through it.

F   You compel me to keep thinking about complex entanglements between cultivation of responsive subjectivities (*askesis*), the diverse efficacies of nonhuman agencies, the bumpiness of planetary forces, the changing regimes of disciplinary power, the lure of truth, the critical role of specific intellectuals and citizens in politics, and the cultivation of courage in the pursuit of truth. I do not demean the pursuit of truth as I might have appeared to do in my early work, since every time a subjugated injury within a regime is exposed, a truth claim is being pursued. I merely thought it wise to defer that question for a while.

I doubt that we would become drinking buddies if we found our way back into the world today. But I appreciate the exploratory, adventurous, creative, and caring persona you cultivate as well as your sense that to come to terms with a new world we need to fold the bumpy trajectories of multiple planetary processes more actively into philosophy, the humanities, the human sciences, and cross-regional citizen activism.

Above all, I concur with you on the need to combat the complementary ways that aggressive denial and passive nihilism short-circuit urgently needed energies today. The task is to cultivate positive strains of attachment to this world partly by forging a new cultural *askesis*, to draw upon those energies to support cross-regional, eco-egalitarian social movements, and to expose and oppose the ugliness predictably brought by many neoliberals and all neofascists against such positive movements. A new fascism is a real danger today.[29] In such a context, critique is both essential and insufficient. Positive action is also imperative.

Notes

Introduction

1 According to a *New York Times* report on July 14, 2018, after the Trump tax cuts of 2018 and amid low unemployment, the percentage of national income received by workers was 62 percent, down from 66 percent in 2000. Corporate profits soared to 13.2 percent, up from 8.3 percent that year. The average worker lost $3,400 during that period. See Cohen, "Corporate Profits Swell." For a study that explores connections between the shifting infrastructure of consumption and the binds facing the working class and more marginal classes, see Connolly, *Capitalism and Christianity*, chapters 4 and 5. Several interim reforms to address those binds are also proposed there.

2 Connolly, *Aspirational Fascism*.

3 I take the terms "major" and "minor" tradition from Gilles Deleuze and Félix Guattari. It is introduced in their *Kafka* and pursued more widely and deeply in *A Thousand Plateaus*. The list of thinkers these two authors call "major" (or sometimes "royal") corresponds rather well to the one Bernard Williams draws up in contrast with Sophocles and Thucydides. A key criterion of distinction for me is whether the thinker acknowledges planetary volatility or not. But the relation of each thinker to a specific mode of explanation, becoming, race, empire, theology, capitalism, and gender are also pertinent to such a cluster concept. Some thinkers slide away from the minor tradition along one or two dimensions while fitting it in others. It is best to speak of

tendencies here, in a world in which the quest for closed definitions is a fool's errand. Contemporary thinkers who participate in the minor tradition are invoked from time to time as the text proceeds.

4 My first essay on this topic was titled "Europe: A Minor Tradition," in Scott and Hirschkind, eds., *Powers of the Secular Modern*. The essay poses a friendly response to Talal Asad, the renowned anthropologist of Christianity and Islam, who argues that the image of modern Europe as a secular continent tends to overemphasize the importance of creed in religious life (which could then be consigned to the private realm) and to underplay the role of ritual, conduct, and mimetic contagion in the quality of religious and cultural life. Those behavioral diversities find public expression in a pluralist society and must not be consigned to a private realm, via the myth of secularism. I concurred with Asad, as I learned from him. But I also contended that there is a minor tradition within European thought itself which challenges the major tradition he reviews; it concurs with him on some of his main points. The examples of minor theorists in that essay were Spinoza, Nietzsche, Stuart Hampshire, and Gilles Deleuze. Here I retain those attributes of the minor tradition and emphasize more appreciation of planetary/cultural imbrications in a world punctuated by planetary volatilities.

5 For attention to the presence and importance of such subordinate themes in major thinkers, see Whitehead, *Process and Reality*, and Holland, *Nomad Citizenship*. The first author plumbs minor themes in Plato, Locke, Hume, and Kant, drawing several of those themes into his own thinking. The second does the same with respect to Marx and Hayek. Marx, again, straddles the two mobile traditions, as do several other thinkers. Holland is out to valorize the minor Marx. Advocates of the minor tradition, focusing on multiple, intersecting temporalities, often drop the themes of necessary progress and linear advance from their images of time.

6 For a fascinating discussion of the difference between Kropotkin on the one hand and Marx on the other with respect to the issue of climate volatility or gradualism, see Davis, *Old Gods, New Enigmas*, chapter 3. He identifies Kropotkin as an early proponent of planetary volatility, a volatility that is not entirely reducible to the effects of civilizational forces.

7 For a discussion of these issues, see Alley, *The Two-Mile Time Machine*, and Broecker, *The Great Ocean Conveyor*. The first is a glaciologist and the second an oceanographer.

8 That task has been launched in chapter 4 of Connolly, *Capitalism and Christianity*, and chapter 3 of Connolly, *Aspirational Fascism*.

9 The post noted below cites the source of some of these charges. A more recent text is McIntyre, *Post-truth*. In a quotation pertinent to the third essay in this study, McIntyre says, "Here we arrive at the second thesis of postmodernism:

that any profession of truth is nothing more than the reflection of the political ideology of the person who is making it. Michel Foucault's idea was that our societal life is defined by language but language is itself is shot through with the relations of power and dominance" (126). A few points are pertinent. First, Foucault explicitly refused the title of postmodernist; the reasons he did so have been widely reviewed. Second, in his middle phase Foucault was concerned particularly with how specific regimes of truth could sustain injurious modes of life, and he examined such regimes in detail in ways that helped to spawn new movements in medical practice, prison reform, sexuality, gender, and the rights of boat people. It would be interesting to know which of the previous regimes McIntyre endorses, whether he embraces the new movements that emerged to challenge them, and what image of truth he himself thinks is best suited to help us negotiate the rocky relations between social disciplines and objectivity. Third, Foucault placed his own conception of truth on hold in his early work but returned to the issue later. It may be that truth is a pursuit that we must take very seriously and that genealogical histories teach us over and over how what was held with great confidence at one time in multiple venues to be true is often believed later to embody a series of destructive untruths. The two parties who form the basis of the dialogue constructed in the third essay—Foucault and Whitehead—both found themselves shocked a few times, as they were pressed to reconsider previous views that they and others had treated as part of a solid regime of truth. McIntyre? What positive philosophy of truth does he advance under the sway of self-modesty?

10 By a neopositivist image, I mean one that plays down the constitutive relation between available testing devices and observable evidence, treats objects of inquiry as fully susceptible to deterministic analysis, eliminates (as a corollary) appreciation of pulses of creativity in most objects of inquiry, and acts as if the progress of science assumes a linear trajectory. Whitehead and Foucault contest such assumptions, while pursuing the lure of truth.

11 Connolly, "Fake News and 'Postmodernism.'"

12 For several decades, the dominant debate in the human sciences was between two parties: first, advocates of social explanation, who sought to identify structural conditions that show how an old regime was determined and to identify new factors that enable change; they were ranged against advocates of cultural interpretation, who emphasized the role of creative agency and played up the importance of language in constituting the intersubjective web of human cultures. Process philosophy challenges a key assumption that tends to bind the two debating partners together: the assumption that culture, agency, and society are reserved to human beings alone. In a world composed of multiple intersecting human and nonhuman agencies of different sorts, interpretation both gains an edge over explanation and forfeits the

story of human exceptionalism often identified with it. In chapter 3, W will be identified with a panexperientialist version of process philosophy; it locates traces of agency everywhere. F gradually accepts that there are multiple agencies of diverse sorts without accepting the panexperientialist idea that agency of some sort or other is operative in all nonhuman processes. This issue also comes up in chapter 1 when we discuss Terrence Deacon's account of the emergence of life from nonlife.

13 Connolly, "Fake News and 'Postmodernism.'"

14 A genealogical analysis is one that seeks to show how entities commonly taken to be singular or eternal are actually composites formed through complex processes involving power assemblages. Nietzsche and Foucault are masters of genealogical analysis, bringing it to bear on Christianity, sexuality, morality, neoliberalism, the subject, truth, and diverse rationalities. Neither would accept the label of "postmodernist," however. Foucault, indeed, publicly refused the label because of the amoralism commonly associated with it and its reputed refusal to pursue positive agendas. Clearly, neither is a relativist either, though some theorists who are themselves confined to only a two-slot set of alternatives love to place Foucault there.

1. Sophocles, Mary Shelley, and the Planetary

1 Williams, *Shame and Necessity*.

2 See Nietzsche, *Twilight of the Idols*. The first moment is operative in Plato, a "real world, attainable to the wise, the pious, the virtuous man." The second finds expression in Paul and Augustine: a world "unattainable for the moment, but promised to . . . the sinner who repents." The third moment is discernible in Kant: the world in itself "cannot be promised, but even when merely thought of, a consolation, a duty an imperative." Here: "The idea grown sublime, pale, northerly, Konigsbergian." If and when you pass beyond the fourth and fifth to the sixth, the real world is abolished and the apparent world is abolished with it too. Is the result nothingness, then, in this Zarathustrian world? No, for now the pair appearance/reality in a dualistic world has been replaced by pluralities of becoming/consolidation in a world taken to be both worthy of human embrace and rather rocky "in itself" (40–41). These pages prefigure the Williams account, though perhaps emphasizing the element in item 6 of plural becomings more than he does.

3 Williams, *Shame and Necessity*, 151.

4 The phrase "majoritarian tradition" or "royal tradition" was composed by Gilles Deleuze and Félix Guattari. In *Kafka*, they contrast a bumpy, minor tradition (composed of thinkers such as Heraclitus, Lucretius, Spinoza, Kafka,

and Nietzsche) with a major tradition composed of the same thinkers identified by Williams. The former thinkers, among other things, stretch and strain dominant tendencies of language in the major tradition. They also typically expose its dangers and subjugations through greater attention to nonhuman forces.

5 Williams, *Shame and Necessity*, 150, 162–63.

6 See Nietzsche, *Thus Spoke Zarathustra*; and Connolly, "Beyond Good and Evil."

7 Sophocles, *Oedipus at Colonus*, in *The Oedipus Plays of Sophocles*, 92–93.

8 Sophocles, *Oedipus at Colonus*, 144, 156.

9 Sophocles, *Oedipus at Colonus*, 168–69 and 169 respectively.

10 Sophocles, *Oedipus at Colonus*, 171.

11 Sophocles, *Oedipus at Colonus*, 176.

12 Sophocles, *Oedipus at Colonus*, 177.

13 I note that in his superb essay on how *Oedipus at Colonus* represents the conflict and subterranean affinities between Thebes and Athens, Pierre Vidal-Naquet does not deal with the natural forces that keep erupting, except for short references to what they may symbolize. I also hesitate to call *Oedipus at Colonus* a tragedy, though Naquet does. It is, rather, the emblematic ending of a life that has revealed a lot about the way of the world and the tragic contingencies it can produce. There is no tragic denouement in this play but rather a drama about the world written by a playwright with a tragic vision of possibility. For Vidal-Naquet's piece, see "Oedipus between Two Cities," in Vernant and Vidal-Naquet, *Myth and Tragedy in Ancient Greece*. My thinking is perhaps closer to de Romilly, *Time in Greek Tragedy*. I am also indebted to studies of a Greek tragic vision by Honig, *Antigone, Interrupted*; and Johnston, *American Dionysia*. In each case, I suspect, closer attention to the planetary dimension is waiting to be addressed.

14 See Chillymanjaro, "Increasing Seismic Activity in Aegean Sea."

15 For a good summary of the event with other references, see "Minoan Eruption," *New World Encyclopedia*.

16 For one fascinating account of philosophers who contested the story of the gods before and during the period in which Sophocles wrote—as well as one that notes the fate of Thera after the volcanic eruption—see Whitmarsh, *Battling the Gods*.

17 Honig, "Is Man a Sabbatical Animal?," extends our awareness of intersections between secular politics and spiritual practices.

18 Keller, *The Face of the Deep*.

19 Pope Francis, *Laudato Si*.

20 This improbable necessity is explored in chapter 5 of Connolly, *Facing the Planetary*, in conjunction with several other works and political actions already pointing in this direction.

21 See West, *Democracy Matters*. "To see the Gospel of Jesus Christ bastardized by imperial Christians and pulverized by Constantinian believers and then exploited by nihilistic elites of the American empire makes my blood boil" (171–72). A reading from within a Whiteheadian theology of Christianity by Catherine Keller expresses numerous affinities to West's perspective. See, for example, Keller, *The Face of the Deep*.

22 An excellent account of the volcanic eruption and the worldwide turbulences set off by it can be found in Wood, *Tambora*. Wood also examines the impacts these changes had on thinkers such as Mary Shelley, Byron, and Percy Shelley, though they did not trace the source of these travails to Tambora. A shorter account can be found in Fagan, *The Little Ice Age*. The eruption occurred during the late stages of the Little Ice Age, deepening its effects for a short period.

23 Wood, *Tambora*, 89.

24 For an account of the worldwide spread of cholera, see Wood, *Tambora*, 86–95.

25 Fagan and Klinger, foreword, ii.

26 Shelley, *The New Annotated Frankenstein*, 158–59.

27 Theweleit, *Male Fantasies*, 2.

28 More recent expressions of such perspectives can be found in Margulis and Sagan, *Acquiring Genomes*; Deacon, *Incomplete Nature*; Kauffman, *Reinventing the Sacred*.

29 This quotation is taken from Fara, "Erasmus Darwin."

30 Darwin, *The Temple of Nature*, 116. Many are aware of how Nietzsche later experimented with a doctrine of eternal return. In some experiments it took the form of long cycles of repetition; in others it assumed the form of the eternal return of the dissonance of the moment out of which new things sometimes emerged.

31 Deacon, *Incomplete Nature*, 167, 142, 277 respectively.

32 Shelley, *The New Annotated Frankenstein*, 105, 128, 314, 260, 262 respectively.

33 See Shelley, *The Necessity of Atheism*. The text begins, "There is no God. This negation must be understood solely to affect a creative Deity. The hypothesis of a pervading spirit, co-eternal with the universe, remains unshaken" (1). Upon Shelley's death, this text was commonly used as a pretext to look forward to his everlasting damnation.

34 Those I would call entangled humanists include Haraway, *Staying with the Trouble*; van Dooren, *Flight Ways*; Bennett, *Vibrant Matter*; Tsing, *The Mushroom at the End of the World*; Nixon, *Slow Violence and the Environmentalism of the Poor*; Keller, *Political Theology of the Earth*; Klein, *This Changes Everything*; Moore, *Capitalism in the Web of Life*; Viveiros de Castro, *Cannibal Metaphysics*.

35 James, *A Pluralistic Universe*; Bergson, *Creative Evolution*; Keller, *The Face of the Deep*.

36 Danowski and Viveiros de Castro launch one such effort in *The Ends of the World*. Anatoli Ignatov forges fecund connections between the thought of the Gurensci in Ghana and Nietzschean themes in "The Earth as Gift-Giving Ancestor." Nietzsche expresses what is here called the minor or eccentric tradition in European thought. I engage Anna Tsing, Rob Nixon, and Dipesh Chakrabarty on these issues in chapter 6 of Connolly, *Facing the Planetary*, "Postcolonial Ecologies, Extinction Events, and Entangled Humanism."

37 Gilles Deleuze and Félix Guattari portray such a minor tradition of thought in *Kafka*. I sometimes call it an eccentric tradition to emphasize the ways it challenges concentric images of family, locality, nation and civilizational circles of resonance, its respect for volatile aspects of the world, and the need to give it more prominence in the humanities and human sciences.

38 This story is superbly told in Benton, *When Life Nearly Died*. I am basically condensing his account into a few paragraphs.

39 To be a shining point, a text must both acknowledge capitalism as a geological force and link that acknowledgment to the periodic volatility of a variety of planetary processes with self-organizing powers of their own. Here are a few studies in journalism, the humanities, and human sciences that do pursue such a combination: Barad, *Meeting the Universe Halfway*; Bennett, *Vibrant Matter*; Morton, *Hyperobjects*; Pearce, *With Speed and Violence*; Grosz, *Chaos, Territory, Art*; Connolly, *The Fragility of Things*; Keller, *Cloud of the Impossible*; Sagan, *Cosmic Apprentice*; Tsing, *The Mushroom at the End of the World*; Fagan, *The Great Warming*.

40 Some of these figures, starting with Alvarez, are discussed in Benton, *When Life Nearly Died*. For others, see Alley, *The Two-Mile Time Machine*; Gould, *The Structure of Evolutionary Theory*; Broecker, *The Great Ocean Conveyor*; Kauffman, *Reinventing the Sacred*; Zalasiewicz and Williams, *Ocean Worlds*.

41 See Gould, *The Structure of Evolutionary Theory*, 1208–18, where he reviews how his theory of tiers of time and punctuated equilibrium in species evolution was preceded by Nietzsche in *On the Genealogy of Morals*. A graduate student pointed this out to Gould late in the day. For an account of Nietzsche's views on this topic, see Connolly, *The Fragility of Things*, chapter 6.

2. The Anthropocene as Abstract Machine

1 Guattari, *The Three Ecologies*. For a thoughtful engagement with Guattari on how the three registers intersect, see Bennett, *Vibrant Matter*, chapter 8.

2 Deleuze and Guattari, *A Thousand Plateaus*, 510 and 511 respectively.

3 Deleuze and Guattari, *A Thousand Plateaus*, 423.

4 "An abstract machine in itself is destratified, deterritorialized; it has no form of its own (much less substance) and makes no distinction within itself between content and expression." Deleuze and Guattari, *A Thousand Plateaus*, 141.

5 For a recent engagement with these issues, see Connolly, "How DOES a Democracy Die?"

6 For a book that sought to diagnose the Trump movement as it was coming to power, see Connolly, *Aspirational Fascism*. The last chapter explores how to pursue egalitarian pluralism and responses to the Anthropocene together in ways that might help to break up the dangerous assemblage Trump has consolidated. It also begins to reshape some of the contending ideals that have competed for hegemony in the twentieth century.

7 For an essay that explains why I call them aspirational fascist movements rather than populist movements, see Connolly, "Populism or Fascism?"

8 See Williams and Srnicek, "#Accelerate." Other essays in that volume are also useful. The best critical engagement with accelerationism I have read to date is Shaviro, *No Speed Limit*. Shaviro, drawing upon both Marx and Deleuze/Guattari, identifies the nihilism and cynicism that can readily occupy accelerationism; he embraces the acceleration of aesthetic drives that contest the bind of a capitalist mobilization of acquisitive desires and their concurrent frustration in old capitalist states.

9 For one statement of needed and potential shifts in the infrastructure and ethos of consumption, see Connolly, *Capitalism and Christianity*, chapter 4. For a politics of swarming that could possibly promote such ends, see Connolly, *Facing the Planetary*, chapter 5.

10 Harper, *The Fate of Rome*.

11 To be more precise, sporadic cooling and droughts started in the fourth century, but the Late Antique Little Ice Age hit most sharply after 530 CE. "We might consider the period ca AD 450–530 the prelude to the Late Antique Little Ice Age" (Harper, *The Fate of Rome*, 251). Harper also reviews the competing views of Justinian and Cassiodorus during this period about the relation of the empire to larger planetary forces. Justinian found the processes to be regular and orderly; Cassiodorus found them to be more volatile. Though I am not independently versed in the thought of Cassiodorus, it sounds like the first thinker fits the major tradition and the latter slides closer to the minor tradition, as those two multifarious traditions have been presented in this text.

12 Harper, *The Fate of Rome*, 155.

13 Harper, *The Fate of Rome*, 277.

14 See Keller, *Political Theology of the Earth*; and Nixey, *The Darkening Age*. Here we have an interesting case of texts that may both reinforce and pass by each other. Keller is superb—here and elsewhere—in reviewing struggles in Chris-

tianity over how to define itself internally and whether to welcome a diversity of faiths. She connects those previous struggles to their import today for attempts to respond to the Anthropocene. Nixey reviews multiple ways and means by which state and Christian terrorism broke the spiritual diversity of the Roman Empire by ransacking temples, intimidating pagans, and killing leaders; but she evinces less sense of anxieties of the time, especially from the period of Justinian on, or how they were tied to climate change and plagues. Harper, Nixey, and Keller speak to one another, each perhaps adding a theme pertinent to the others.

15 Harper, *The Fate of Rome*, 248.

16 Harper, *The Fate of Rome*, 254.

17 This story is well told by Benton, *When Life Nearly Died*.

18 I refer above all to Keller, *Political Theology of the Earth*, but also to Keller's earlier book, *The Face of the Deep*. For Pope Francis, see *Laudato Si*.

19 I begin such engagements in Connolly, *Facing the Planetary*. Keller in *Political Theology of the Earth*; Danowski and Viveiros de Castro in *The Ends of the World*; and Singh in *Poverty and the Quest for Life* join others in digging deeper. For another superb essay that places African animism in close conversation with Nietzschean thought, see Ignatov, "The Earth as Gift-Giving Ancestor."

20 Moore, *Capitalism in the Web of Life*.

21 It is a little discouraging to read in Brannen, *The Ends of the World*, how Amerindians twelve thousand years ago probably wiped out a set of large mammals such as mastodons. That does not detract, however, from the profound sense of eco-responsibility indigenous peoples pursue and teach others today in opposition to predatory capitalism. It, rather, shows how in many times and places people have not quite known what they were doing.

22 See Watts, "Domino-Effect of Climate Events."

23 For a thoughtful discussion of early European settler misunderstandings of the changing climate on the continent they invaded, see White, *A Cold Welcome*. White does not focus much on how various Amerindian peoples themselves coped with the combination of climate pressure and European invasions.

24 I am not denying of course that a forcing does not itself act as a trigger often enough, setting off amplifiers. That was certainly the case in some of the early planetary shifts before the rise of human civilizations. The rough and ready distinctions between forcings, drivers, triggers, and amplifiers suggested here are for the purposes of preliminary orientation, helping us to see, for instance, how and why parallelism is an unwise assumption.

25 In Connolly, *Capitalism and Christianity*, chapter 4, I explore a series of interim adjustments that could be launched today in old capitalist states, if the resistances could be surmounted from fossil fuel companies, finance capital,

white evangelicals, the Republican Party, and white working-class constituencies who believe their future is tied to extractive practices.

26 I pursue the cross-regional politics of swarming in Connolly, *Facing the Planetary*, chapter 5. The point now is to see how the danger of fascism grows as delays in promoting such an agenda continue.

3. The Lure of Truth

1 At this point, a few might seek to short-circuit the inquiry launched here by saying that it is essential to engage a variety of non-Western cultures that have been placed under the gun of Euro-American imperialism—yes, as I began to do in Connolly, *Facing the Planetary*, chapter 6, "Postcolonial Ecologies, Extinction Events, and Entangled Humanism." But since some decolonizing constituencies themselves advance versions of either panexperientialism or species perspectivalism, the point may be to do so in ways that do not efface acknowledgment of multiple subjectivities beyond the human. One impressive thing about Danowski and Viveiros de Castro, *The Ends of the World*, is how they keep both these issues alive. So does Viveiros de Castro himself in *Cannibal Metaphysics*, a book that moves back and forth between the minor philosophy of Deleuze on one hand and the perspectivalism of Amazonians on the other. The idea is to be alert to each enterprise in ways that do not short-circuit the other. The dialogue here attends to a mix of disciplinary and ontological possibilities emanating from a minor tradition in Euro-American philosophy that both supports the Danowski/Viveiros de Castro project and breaks down assumptions in dominant Euro-American social sciences that diminish the role of nonhuman processes of multiple types in the interior of social life. The breakdown of the latter prejudice is important in itself and, perhaps, a useful aid to further explorations back and forth between Euro-American and other traditions.

2 For an account of this issue in the context of the Trump administration, see Connolly, "Fake News and 'Postmodernism.'" The argument there is to fend off fake news, promote and respect the search for evidence that bears upon claims, and also appreciate the role that real creativity plays in being.

3 Foucault, *Herculine Barbin*. Foucault begins his brief introduction to this collection of the memoir, journalistic exposés, doctors' reports, legal judgments, and priestly commentaries with this statement: "Do we *truly* need a *true* sex?" (vii). Perhaps we could today ask, "Do we *truly* need a *true* identity?" The upshot is that we need both identities and to come to terms positively with their contingent elements and their entanglements with other identities. The proliferation of LGBTQ movements today shows how a pluralization of sexual

identities is possible; it also suggests how related movements in domains such as religious faith, ethnic crossings, and racial categories involve shifts in behavioral norms, political struggles, medical practices, and relational expectations. The politics of pluralization, indeed, discloses the social and bodily layering of established norms of gender duality as it challenges the established sense of necessity folded into the layers.

4 In responding to the demand of Francis Bacon to suppress speculation and simply to extrapolate laws from an accumulation of facts, Whitehead says, "Unfortunately for this objection [to philosophical speculation] there are no brute, self-contained matters of fact, capable of being understood apart from interpretation as an element of a system. Whenever we attempt to express the matter of immediate experience we find that its understanding leads us beyond itself, to its contemporaries, to its past, to its future and to the universals in terms of which its definiteness is exhibited" (*Process and Reality*, 14).

5 As far as I know, Whitehead did not discuss Nietzsche in print, though the latter was of course very important to Foucault. However, an old copy of *The Will to Power* marked up by Whitehead has recently been discovered. I now own a pdf of that copy. The markings often focus on nodules where Nietzsche explores panexperientialism (a doctrine that Whitehead and Nietzsche shared) and a few where he thinks about the subterranean influences of old theologies on scientific doctrines that purport to break cleanly with them.

6 For a superb review of these changes, and the challenges they face, see Quammen, *The Tangled Tree*. Whitehead would hold these processes to be populated with a series of intersecting microagents. Creativity, such as the emergence of a new species, periodically emerges out of such horizontal intersections. The Quammen review of how a recent regime of truth was held together in evolutionary biology, only to crack through a rapid turn led by speculative thinkers and the production of new tests, provides an interesting history of the interdependence between a regime and lures of truth in one domain. It does not resolve the differences between F and W on this issue, however.

7 For Whitehead's engagement with romanticism as a route to overcome some of the closures and dualities of classical science, see his *Science and the Modern World*, chapter 5, "The Romantic Reaction." F will soon accuse him of being closer to a romantic image of the world's drive to translate incompatibilities into harmonized contrasts than he probably took himself to be. But, remember, the relevant terms of comparison here are not merely between Whitehead and romanticism but also between Whitehead's image and Foucault's of a dangerous world.

8 "We must not imagine that the world . . . is the accomplice of our knowledge; there is no prediscursive providence which predisposes the world in our favor" (Foucault, "The Order of Discourse," 68). This text was composed

before Foucault began to focus more intensively on the composition of the subject and the manifold tactics by which it could become more responsive.

9 For an evidence-based speculation that this did happen, see chapter 8 in Margulis and Sagan, *Dazzle Gradually*. Lynn Margulis is also the biologist who discovered the formation of nucleated bacteria through horizontal evolution.

10 As Whitehead says, the "searchlight of consciousness" is weak, and misses "millions upon millions of centers of life in each animal body." Experience exceeds consciousness in part because it responds to those agencies (Whitehead, *Process and Reality*, 108).

11 See, for example, Mayer, *The Mind-Gut Connection*. The author emphasizes how the gut, replete with its own cortical organization and filled with bacteria and hormones, both influences behavior itself and enters into complex exchanges with the brain systems in the head. Our moods, intuitions, dispositions, and tendencies to judgment are profoundly influenced by these processes. Whitehead would call many of the agencies involved microsubjects. This book is full of riches for a Whiteheadian perspective. Earlier theories of brain processes took a much more mechanical view of brain processes. Moreover, Foucault's explorations of "tactics of the self" are designed to work upon such processes below the level of conscious awareness.

12 "A feeling bears on itself the scars of its birth; it retains the impress of what might have been but is not. It is for this reason that what an actual entity has avoided as a datum for feeling may be an important part of its equipment." So "the actual cannot be reduced to mere matter of fact in divorce from its potential" (Whitehead, *Process and Reality*, 226–27).

13 Foucault, shortly after the first volume on sexuality was finished, explored LSD as a way to loosen up the pores of subjectivity. See Jones, "When Michel Foucault Tripped on Acid." I thank Jairus Grove for calling this to my attention. A recent book by Pollan, *How to Change Your Mind*, reviews research in neuroscience and psychotherapy with psilocybin, the active ingredient in psychedelic mushrooms. The studies, renewed cautiously after the cultural fiascoes and right-wing attacks of the 1960s, suggest that in controlled settings and doses, default modes of contained thinking tend to open up, rendering subjects more exploratory and affirmative. Suppressed lines of communication between different brain regions—closures needed to promote action-oriented perception—become open again. Do the effects last? The speculation is that they may last if mindfulness practices continue after the clinical injections. This is all still experimental. For a discussion of William James on drugs, mindfulness, and mystical experience, see Connolly, *Neuropolitics*. The self-avowed debt of Whitehead to James makes this line of communication between F and W all the more pertinent. *Neuropolitics* also speculates about the importance of brain/gut communications, which became more prominent in neuroscience experiments later.

14 A systematic theory is one that takes each of its elements to be logically implied by the others, the whole to be set in a series of transcendental arguments, and the complex to be vindicated by empirical evidence. Both Foucault and Whitehead resisted the hubris of that agenda. This comes out in Whitehead's critique of the power of transcendental arguments and his expectation that an element of speculation, though its edges do shift, is apt to be ineliminable from theory and philosophy. For Foucault's view, see "Polemics, Politics and Problematizations." Indeed, the psilocybin experiments noted earlier are pertinent here too. For these experiments cannot, by their very nature, be blind because patients feel the effects of the drug and thus know they were not given a placebo and because the effects cannot be sharply divorced from subjective reports of experience either. Experimentalism now takes on a more open quality, as James, Foucault, and Whitehead all thought it should.

15 Transcendental arguments can take different forms. In one basic format you first establish that something is indubitable in experience, then ascertain what must be presupposed by that experience, then treat those latter presuppositions as basic postulates of epistemology and morality. Foucault's and Whitehead's objections to the necessity of many transcendental arguments are, first, that the "indubitable" features of experience are often more vague and filled with pluripotentialities than these arguments acknowledge, and, second, that the argument depends upon an analytic/synthetic dichotomy that is unnecessary to logic as such and is too crude to capture the subtleties of experience.

16 Whitehead uses the terms "correct" and "truth" in ways that could complicate the above formulation. To stick with the second term for now, one could say that you speculate it to be a metaphysical truth that the world is populated with bouts of real creativity. That would then mean that truth in a more mundane sense as a correct reading of entities in the world could change from time to time. To keep the terminology more or less familiar in this dialogue, I will stick with this formulation of a distinction between modes of truth.

17 A more thorough engagement with Foucault himself would consult closely his last, profound set of lectures, published as Foucault, *The Courage of Truth*. Here Foucault, engaging the ancient Greeks, explores relays back and forth between the pursuit of truth, preparing the soul to engage it, and preparing the self to have the courage to express it under conditions of danger. I hope to further address this fecund text soon. For now it may be enough to suggest that Foucault and Whitehead both explored the pursuit of truth and the courage of truth.

18 "And even if I won't say that what is characterized as 'Schizophrenia' *corresponds* to something real in the world, this has nothing to do with idealism. For I think there is a relation between the thing which is problematized and the

process of problematization. The problematization is an 'answer' to a concrete situation which is real" (Foucault, *Fearless Speech*, 171–72, emphasis added).

19 For an exploration of the role of conceptual personae in philosophy, see Deleuze and Guattari, *What Is Philosophy?*, 61–85. Deleuze and Guattari would include both Foucault and Whitehead in the minor tradition of European philosophy, which challenges much in the major tradition and rejects its drives to imperialism.

20 Whitehead is typically taken to be an advocate of panexperientialism or panpsychism, the view that all entities express differential capacities of striving and experience, even though some large processes wash out microagencies within them. However, in *Modes of Thought*, he may qualify that view when he talks about how the *liveliness* of inorganic processes evolves into *living* processes. Foucault in his middle phase is apt to have held a view that only vertebrates have complex capacities of striving and experience. In this dialogue, however, F is projected to arrive at a subtle view about the emergence of life from nonlife. Such a view is more feasible than classical images of emergence because the liveliness of a quantum world makes it more possible for life to emerge from it. As noted in chapter 1, a promising version of the latter view is advanced by Terrence Deacon in *Incomplete Nature*, when he projects how two separate clusters of complex molecules resonated together to spawn a product—life with reproductive powers—that neither could spawn alone. That version of the emergence thesis is discussed in chapter 1.

21 Foucault: "I like the word ['curiosity']; it evokes the care one takes of what exists and might exist; a sharpened sense of reality, but one that is never immobilized before it; a readiness to find what surrounds us strange and odd; a certain determination to throw off familiar ways of thought and to look at the same things in a different way . . . ; a lack of respect for the traditional hierarchies of what is important and fundamental" (Foucault, "The Masked Philosopher," 328).

22 "The important thing here, I believe, is that truth isn't outside power, or lacking in power: contrary to a myth whose history and functions would repay further study, truth isn't the reward of free spirits, the child of protracted solitude, nor the privilege of those who have succeeded in liberating themselves. Each society has its regime of truth, its general politics of truth . . . the mechanisms and instances which enable one to distinguish true and false statements, the means by which each is sanctioned, the techniques and procedures accorded value in the acquisition of truth; the status of those who are charged with saying what is true" (Foucault, *Power/Knowledge*, 131).

23 It might be that F's suggestion here is that W, writing during an early period of the quantum revolution, was in fact closer to the later interpretation of quantum mechanics advanced by David Bohm than he should have been. See Bohm, *Wholeness and the Implicate Order*.

24 In Whitehead, *Process and Reality*, the oft-repeated phrase "creative advance" is open to more than one interpretation. When he emphasizes how previous incompatibilities are transfigured into harmonies of contrast that enable more complex entities to come into being, it sounds like the world during "this cosmic epoch" is progressing toward greater complexity. But such phrases are punctuated by discussions of periods of "chaotic disorder" and statements such as the following: "Thus all societies require interplay with their environment and in the case of living societies this interplay takes the form of robbery" (105). While it is debatable what the balances were in Whitehead (not speaking now to the position W begins to take in this dialogue), one theme does tend to persist. While "decay" sets in because "laws" are always imperfect and run into resistances, changes in planetary processes do seem to be gradual for him. The new planetary sciences challenge planetary gradualism by identifying several deep, sometimes rapid, changes in the history of the planet.

25 For Foucault's prescient engagements with neoliberalism, see Foucault, *The Birth of Biopolitics*. For a superb study that explores the interlocked disinformation campaigns in this domain by scientists tied to fossil fuel companies, see Oreskes and Conway, *Merchants of Doubt*.

26 I discuss aggressive nihilism and passive nihilism with respect to the Anthropocene in Connolly, *Facing the Planetary*, 162–68.

27 For my own efforts to articulate a political strategy—and interim policies connected to it—see *Capitalism and Christianity*, chapter 4, and *Facing The Planetary*, chapters 5 and 6. Those books do not respond to the issue of population, in part because the proposals are for interim measures. Given the ugly colonial and racist history of several state population policies, perhaps the best approach is to provide birth control information and general opportunities, reversing general policies to promote fecundity that have prevailed in many state and religious regimes while refusing any coercive approach.

28 This list of items is fairly close to one Whitehead himself draws up in chapter 3 of *The Function of Reason*. He also advances a critique of market theories of the economy in that little book.

29 In Foucault, *Language, Counter-memory, Practice*, Foucault and Deleuze entered into a dialogue in 1972 on power and activism. At one juncture, Deleuze said, "We cannot shut out the scream of Reich: the masses were not deceived: at a particular time, they actually wanted a fascist regime! There are investments of desire that mold and distribute power, that make it the property of the policeman as much as the prime minister moment" (215). Both Foucault and Deleuze played up in that piece the recurrent rise of fascist passions. In that book, however, Foucault resisted pursuing a positive vision, a resistance he overcame in his late work.

Bibliography

Alley, Richard B. *The Two-Mile Time Machine: Ice Cores, Abrupt Climate Change and Our Future*. Princeton, NJ: Princeton University Press, 2000.

Barad, Karen. *Meeting the Universe Halfway: Quantum Physics and the Entanglement of Matter and Meaning*. Durham, NC: Duke University Press, 2007.

Bennett, Jane. *Vibrant Matter: A Political Ecology of Things*. Durham, NC: Duke University Press, 2010.

Benton, Michael. *When Life Nearly Died: The Greatest Mass Extinction of All Time*. New York: Thames and Hudson, 2005.

Bergson, Henri. *Creative Evolution*. Translated by Arthur Mitchell. Mineola, NY: Dover, 1998.

Bohm, David. *Wholeness and the Implicate Order*. New York: Routledge, 1988.

Brannen, Peter. *The Ends of the World: Volcanic Apocalypses, Lethal Oceans and Our Quest to Understand Earth's Past Mass Extinctions*. New York: HarperCollins, 2017.

Broecker, Wally. *The Great Ocean Conveyor: Discovering the Trigger for Abrupt Climate Change*. Princeton, NJ: Princeton University Press, 2010.

Chillymanjaro. "Increasing Seismic Activity in Aegean Sea (with Tectonic Summary)." *The Watchers*, January 28, 2012. https://watchers.news/2012/01/28/increasing-seismic-activities-in-aegean-sea-greece-with-tectonic-summary/.

Cohen, Patricia. "Corporate Profits Swell, but Workers See No Relief." *New York Times*, July 14, 2008.

Connolly, William E. *Aspirational Fascism: The Struggle for Multifaceted Democracy under Trumpism*. Minneapolis: University of Minnesota Press, 2017.

Connolly, William E. "Beyond Good and Evil: The Ethical Sensibility of Michel Foucault." *Political Theory* 21, no. 3 (1993): 365–89.

Connolly, William E. *Capitalism and Christianity, American Style*. Durham, NC: Duke University Press, 2008.

Connolly, William E. "Europe: A Minor Tradition." In *Powers of the Secular Modern: Talal Asad and His Interlocutors*, edited by David Scott and Charles Hirschkind, 75–92. Stanford, CA: Stanford University Press, 2006.

Connolly, William E. *Facing the Planetary: Entangled Humanism and the Politics of Swarming*. Durham, NC: Duke University Press, 2017.

Connolly, William E. "Fake News and 'Postmodernism': The Fake Equation." *The Contemporary Condition*, May 5, 2018. http://contemporarycondition .blogspot.com/2018/05/fake-news-and-postmodernism-fake.html.

Connolly, William E. *The Fragility of Things: Self-Organizing Processes, Neoliberal Fantasies, and Democratic Activism*. Durham, NC: Duke University Press, 2013.

Connolly, William E. "How DOES a Democracy Die?" *The Contemporary Condition*, October 9, 2018. http://contemporarycondition.blogspot.com/2018/10/how -does-democracy-die.html.

Connolly, William E. *Neuropolitics: Thinking, Culture, Speed*. Minneapolis: University of Minnesota Press, 2002.

Connolly, William E. "Populism or Fascism?" *The Contemporary Condition*, June 17, 2018. http://contemporarycondition.blogspot.com/2018/06 /populism-or-fascism.html.

Danowski, Déborah, and Eduardo Batalha Viveiros de Castro. *The Ends of the World*. Translated by Rodrigo Nunes. Cambridge, UK: Polity, 2017.

Darwin, Erasmus. *The Temple of Nature: Or, The Origin of Society. A Poem with Philosophical Notes*. 1803. Reprint, Sweden: Timaios Press, 2013.

Davis, Mike. *Old Gods, New Enigmas: Marx's Lost Theory*. London: Verso, 2018.

Deacon, Terrence W. *Incomplete Nature: How Mind Emerged from Matter*. New York: Norton, 2012.

Deleuze, Gilles, and Félix Guattari. *Kafka: Toward a Minor Literature*. Translated by Dana Polan. Minneapolis: University of Minnesota Press, 1986.

Deleuze, Gilles, and Félix Guattari. *A Thousand Plateaus: Capitalism and Schizophrenia*. Translated by Brian Massumi. Minneapolis: University of Minnesota Press, 1987.

Deleuze, Gilles, and Félix Guattari. *What Is Philosophy?* Translated by Hugh Tomlinson and Graham Burchell. New York: Columbia University Press, 1994.

de Romilly, Jacqueline. *Time in Greek Tragedy*. Ithaca, NY: Cornell University Press, 1968.

Fagan, Brian. *The Great Warming: Climate Change and the Rise and Fall of Civilizations*. London: Bloomsbury, 2008.

Fagan, Brian. *The Little Ice Age: How Climate Made History, 1300–1850*. New York: Basic Books, 2000.

Fara, Patricia. "Erasmus Darwin." *Encyclopedia Britannica*. 2018. https://www.britannica.com/biography/Erasmus-Darwin.

Foucault, Michel. *The Birth of Biopolitics: Lectures at the Collège de France, 1978–79*. Translated by Graham Burchell. Edited by Michel Senellart. New York: Palgrave Macmillan, 2008.

Foucault, Michel. *The Courage of Truth: Lectures at the Collège de France, 1983–84*. Translated by Graham Burchell. New York: Picador, 2012.

Foucault, Michel. *Fearless Speech*. Edited by Joseph Pearson. Los Angeles: Semiotexte, 2001.

Foucault, Michel. *Herculine Barbin: Being the Recently Discovered Memoirs of a Nineteenth-Century French Hermaphrodite*. Translated by Richard McDougal. New York: Pantheon, 1980.

Foucault, Michel. *Language, Counter-memory, Practice: Selected Essays and Interviews*. Edited by Donald Bouchard. Translated by Donald Bouchard and Sherry Simon. Oxford: Basil Blackwell, 1977.

Foucault, Michel. "The Masked Philosopher." In *Politics, Philosophy, Culture: Interviews and Other Writings, 1977–1984*, edited by Lawrence D. Kritzman, 323–30. New York: Routledge, 1988.

Foucault, Michel. "The Order of Discourse." In *Untying the Text: A Poststructuralist Reader*, edited by Robert Young, 48–78. Boston: Routledge and Kegan, 1981.

Foucault, Michel. "Polemics, Politics and Problematizations: An Interview with Michel Foucault." In *The Foucault Reader*, edited by Paul Rabinow, 381–90. New York: Pantheon, 1984.

Foucault, Michel. *Power/Knowledge: Selected Interviews and Other Writings, 1972–1977*. Translated and edited by Colin Gordon. New York: Pantheon, 1980.

Gould, Stephen Jay. *The Structure of Evolutionary Theory*. Cambridge, MA: Harvard University Press, 2002.

Grosz, Elizabeth. *Chaos, Territory, Art: Deleuze and the Framing of the Earth*. New York: Columbia University Press, 2008.

Guattari, Félix. *The Three Ecologies*. Translated by Ian Pindar and Paul Sutton. London: Athlone, 2000.

Haraway, Donna J. *Staying with the Trouble: Making Kin in the Chthulucene*. Durham, NC: Duke University Press, 2016.

Harper, Kyle. *The Fate of Rome: Climate, Disease, and the End of an Empire*. Princeton, NJ: Princeton University Press, 2017.

Holland, Eugene. *Nomad Citizenship: Free Market Communism and the Slow-Motion General Strike*. Minneapolis: University of Minnesota Press, 2011.

Honig, Bonnie. *Antigone, Interrupted*. Cambridge: Cambridge University Press, 2013.

Honig, Bonnie. "Is Man a Sabbatical Animal? Agamben, Heschel and Rosenzweig." Paper presented at the Annual Political Science Association Convention, Philadelphia, September 1–4, 2016.

Ignatov, Anatoli. "The Earth as Gift-Giving Ancestor: Nietzsche's Perspectivism and African Animism." *Political Theory* 45, no. 1 (2017): 52–75.

Ignatov, Anatoli. "Ecologies of the Good Life: Forces, Bodies and Cross Cultural Encounters." PhD diss., Johns Hopkins University, 2014.

James, William. *A Pluralistic Universe*. Lincoln: University of Nebraska Press, 1996.

Johnston, Steven. *American Dionysia: Violence, Tragedy, and Democratic Politics*. Cambridge: Cambridge University Press, 2015.

Jones, Josh. "When Michel Foucault Tripped on Acid in Death Valley and Called It 'the Greatest Experience of My Life' (1975)." *Open Culture*, September 15, 2017. http://www.openculture.com/2017/09/when-michel-foucault-tripped-on-acid -in-death-valley-and-called-it-the-greatest-experience-of-my-life-1975.html.

Kauffman, Stuart. *Reinventing the Sacred: A New View of Science, Reason and Religion*. New York: Basic Books, 2008.

Keller, Catherine. *Cloud of the Impossible: Negative Theology and Planetary Entanglement*. New York: Columbia University Press, 2014.

Keller, Catherine. *The Face of the Deep: A Theology of Becoming*. New York: Routledge, 2003.

Keller, Catherine. *Political Theology of the Earth: Our Planetary Emergency and the Struggle for a New Public*. New York: Columbia University Press, 2018.

Klinger, Leslie S. Foreword to *The New Annotated Frankenstein*, by Mary Shelley, edited by Leslie S. Klinger, xx–lxxii. New York: Norton, 2017.

Klein, Naomi. *This Changes Everything: Capitalism vs. the Climate*. New York: Simon and Schuster, 2014.

Margulis, Lynn. "Spirochetes Awake: Syphilis and Nietzsche's Mad Genius." In *Dazzle Gradually: Reflections on the Nature of Nature*, edited by Lynn Margulis and Dorion Sagan, 57–69. White River Junction, VT: Chelsea Green, 2007.

Margulis, Lynn, and Dorion Sagan. *Acquiring Genomes: A Theory of the Origins of Species*. New York: Basic Books, 2002.

Margulis, Lynn, and Dorion Sagan, eds. *Dazzle Gradually: Reflections on the Nature of Nature*. White River Junction, VT: Chelsea Green, 2007.

Mayer, Emeran. *The Mind-Gut Connection: How the Hidden Conversation within Our Bodies Impacts Our Mood, Our Choices, and Our Overall Health*. New York: Harper and Row, 2016.

McIntyre, Lee. *Post-truth*. Cambridge, MA: MIT Press, 2018.

"Minoan Eruption." *New World Encyclopedia*. 2016. Accessed October 12, 2018. http://www.newworldencyclopedia.org/entry/Minoan_eruption/.

Moore, Jason. *Capitalism in the Web of Life: Ecology and the Accumulation of Capital*. London: Verso, 2015.

Morton, Tim. *Hyperobjects: Philosophy and Ecology after the End of the World*. Minneapolis: University of Minnesota Press, 2013.

Nietzsche, Friedrich. *On the Genealogy of Morals*. Translated by Walter Kaufmann and R. J. Hollingdale. New York: Vintage, 1967.

Nietzsche, Friedrich. *Thus Spoke Zarathustra*. Translated by Walter Kaufmann. New York: Vintage, 1968.

Nietzsche, Friedrich. *Twilight of the Idols*. Translated by R. J. Hollingdale. New York: Penguin, 1968.

Nixey, Catherine. *The Darkening Age: The Christian Destruction of the Classical World*. Boston: Houghton Mifflin Harcourt, 2018.

Nixon, Rob. *Slow Violence and the Environmentalism of the Poor*. Cambridge, MA: Harvard University Press, 2011.

Oreskes, Naomi, and Erik Conway. *Merchants of Doubt: How a Handful of Scientists Obscured the Truth on Issues from Tobacco Smoke to Global Warming*. New York: Bloomsbury, 2011.

Pearce, Fred. *With Speed and Violence: Why Scientists Fear Tipping Points in Climate Change*. Boston: Beacon, 2007.

Pollan, Michael. *How to Change Your Mind: What the New Science of Psychedelics Teaches Us about Consciousness, Dying, Addiction, Depression, and Transcendence*. New York: Penguin, 2018.

Pope Francis. *Laudato Si: On Care for Our Common Home*. Vatican City: Liberia Editrice Vaticana, 2015.

Quammen, David. *The Tangled Tree: A Radical New History of Life*. New York: Simon and Schuster, 2018.

Sagan, Dorion. *Cosmic Apprentice: Dispatches from the Edges of Science*. Minneapolis: University of Minnesota Press, 2013.

Shaviro, Steven. *No Speed Limit: Three Essays on Accelerationism*. Minneapolis: University of Minnesota Press, 2015.

Shelley, Mary. *The New Annotated Frankenstein*. Edited by Leslie S. Klinger. New York: Norton, 2017.

Shelley, Percy. *The Necessity of Atheism*. CreateSpace, 2016.

Singh, Bhrigupati. *Poverty and the Quest for Life: Spiritual and Material Striving in Rural India*. Chicago: University of Chicago Press, 2015.

Sophocles. *The Oedipus Plays of Sophocles: Oedipus the King, Oedipus at Colonus, Antigone*. Translated by Paul Roche. London: Plume, 1996.

Theweleit, Klaus. *Male Fantasies*. Vol. 2, *Male Bodies, Psychoanalyzing the White Terror*. Translated by Erica Carter and Chris Turner. Minneapolis: University of Minnesota Press, 1988.

Tsing, Anna Lowenhaupt. *The Mushroom at the End of the World: On the Possibility of Life in Capitalist Ruins*. Princeton, NJ: Princeton University Press, 2015.

van Dooren, Thom. *Flight Ways: Life and Loss at the Edge of Extinction*. New York: Columbia University Press, 2014.

Vernant, Jean-Pierre, and Pierre Vidal-Naquet. *Myth and Tragedy in Ancient Greece*. Translated by Janet Lloyd. New York: Zone, 1988.

Viveiros de Castro, Eduardo Batalha. *Cannibal Metaphysics*. Translated by Peter Skafish. Minneapolis: Univocal Press, 2014.

Watts, Jonathan. "Domino-Effect of Climate Events Could Move Earth into a 'Hothouse' State." *The Guardian*, August 7, 2018. https://www.theguardian .com/environment/2018/aug/06/domino-effect-of-climate-events-could -push-earth-into-a-hothouse-state.

West, Cornel. *Democracy Matters: Winning the Fight against Imperialism*. New York: Penguin, 2005.

White, Sam. *A Cold Welcome: The Little Ice Age and Europe's Encounter with North America*. Cambridge, MA: Harvard University Press, 2017.

Whitehead, Alfred North. *Dialogues of Alfred North Whitehead*. Edited by Lucien Price. 1954. Reprint, Boston: David R. Godine, 2001.

Whitehead, Alfred North. *The Function of Reason*. Princeton, NJ: Princeton University Press, 1929.

Whitehead, Alfred North. *Modes of Thought*. New York: Cambridge University Press, 1938.

Whitehead, Alfred North. *Process and Reality: An Essay in Cosmology*. Edited by David R. Griffin and Donald W. Sherburne. 1929. Reprint, New York: Free Press, 1978.

Whitehead, Alfred North. *Science and the Modern World*. New York: Free Press, 1925.

Whitmarsh, Tim. *Battling the Gods: Atheism in the Ancient World*. New York: Random House, 2015.

Williams, Alex, and Nick Srnicek. "#Accelerate: Manifesto for an Accelerationalist Politics." In *#Accelerate: The Accelerationist Reader*, edited by Robin Mackay and Armen Avanessian, 347–62. Falmouth, UK: Urbanomic, 2014.

Williams, Bernard. *Shame and Necessity*. Berkeley: University of California Press, 1993.

Wood, Gillen D'Arcy. *Tambora: The Eruption That Changed the World*. Princeton, NJ: Princeton University Press, 2014.

Zalasiewicz, Jan, and Mark Williams. *Ocean Worlds: The Story of Seas on Earth and Other Planets*. Oxford: Oxford University Press, 2014.

Index

capitalism, 2, 15, 35, 42, 61, 64, 88; as axiomatic, 51; and democracy, 62; and fascism, 7–9, 52–55, 62; and fossil extraction, 4, 6–9, 39, 47, 52, 54, 63, 66, 69, 81, 93; as geological era, 63–64; as geological force, 39, 44–47, 55, 62–65, 105n39; and planetary volatility, 8, 51–52; as trigger to climate change, 7, 43–45, 66–67, 90–91, 94; varieties of, 51–55

Capitalocene, 8, 62–65

causality: and cascading processes, 65–69; and force, 7; and heterogenous connections, 6–7, 49–50, 58; as loose relays, 60

Christianity: Constantinian tradition, 25, 43, 56–57, 59–61, 86; and the fall of Rome, 56–59; providentialism, 38, 46. See also fall of Rome; Pope Francis

climate change, 1–3, 14, 25, 40–42, 59, 94; and fascism, 52–53; and Rome, 56–60; triggers to, 23, 43–45, 47, 63, 67–70, 90–91. See also abstract machine; Anthropocene

climate denialism, 2, 43, 45, 53; in neoliberal capitalism, 55, 62–63, 67, 94–95

climate parallelism, assumption of, 8, 62, 107n24

Connolly, William E., 99n1, 105n36, 113n26; on political action, 103n20, 106n9, 107–8n25, 108n26; on Trump and (neo)fascism, 100n8, 106n6, 106n7, 108n2

consumption: abundance of, 39, 47, 64; ethos of, 54, 61, 70, 92, 106n9; infrastructures of, 8–9, 51, 66, 70, 99n1

creativity, 11–12, 14–15, 73; Foucault on, 78; harmonization and, 82–84; and lure of truth, 77–78, 86–89, 96; and scars of the past, 83–85

Danowski, Déborah, and Eduardo B. Viveiros de Castro, 105n36, 108n1

Darwin, Charles, 38, 43, 46; neo-Darwinism, 15, 31, 33, 78–79

Darwin, Erasmus, 30–33, 35, 38

Deacon, Terrence, and evolution, 32–33, 38

Deleuze, Gilles, 42, 91; and Foucault, 113n29

Deleuze, Gilles, and Félix Guattari: abstract machine, 6, 49–50, 106n4; axiomatic, 51; major and minor tradition, 6, 42, 99n3, 102n4, 105n37, 112n19; on nonhuman agency, 47, 49, 103n4; and planetary volatility, 47–48; smooth and striated space, 48

democracy: and fascism, 62; and the minor traditions, 60–61

entanglement, 19, 27, 35, 47; entangled humanism, 40–41, 44, 89, 97; Foucault on, 84, 97, 108n3; Whitehead on, 75, 77

environmentalism, 2

Eternal Sunshine of the Spotless Mind, 76–77

ethic of cultivation, 4, 73; in Foucault, 86, 89, 97. See also presumptive generosity

Eurocentrism, 3, 80, 87, 90–92. See also human exceptionalism; sociocentrism

evangelicalism, 1, 50, 54, 59

evangelical/neoliberal resonance machine, 54–55, 63–64, 67

evolution: Erasmus Darwin, 31–33, 38; horizontal, 49, 79, 82–83, 110n9; human, 28, 34, 39–40, species, 30–31, 34–38, 65; Terrence Deacon, 32–33. See also self-organizing processes

existential dispositions, and politics, 63–64, 81–82, 85–86

fall of Rome, 8, 107n14; and climate conditions, 56–59, 63, 65, 67. See also Harper, Kyle

fascism, 1–3, 11, 61, 71, 85, 97;
    aspirational, 16, 52–54, 62, 106n7;
    and capitalism, 62; and climate
    events, 9, 52–53
forcings, climate, 50, 65; and amplifiers,
    67–69
Foucault, Michel: and Deleuze, 113n29;
    ethics of presumptive care, 16, 85,
    88–90; on gender duality, 74–77; on
    genealogy, 13, 74, 83, 102n14; and
    LSD, 110n13; and McIntyre, 100n9;
    on neoliberalism, 113n25; against
    neopositivism, 101n9; and Nietzsche,
    19, 73, 89, 102n14; and nonhuman
    agency, 79–82, 88, 101n12; power/
    knowledge regimes and resistance,
    81, 84–86; regimes of truth, 4, 13,
    74, 85, 101n9; techniques of the
    self, 78, 80, 85, 110n11; truth and
    power, 73, 112n22; and volatile
    planetary processes, 90–91, 96; and
    Whitehead, 13, 16, 72–97, 111n14;
    will to truth, 73–74, 88, 97

gender duality, 14, 109n3; Foucault on,
    74–77; Whitehead on, 77–78
genealogy, 85; Foucault on, 13, 74,
    101n9, 102n14
God, 32–34, 54, 59; Greek gods, 3,
    17–22, 24, 41, 94, 103n16; limited,
    24, 41, 60; omnipotence, 4, 34–35,
    38–39, 56–57, 77, 86
Golden Age, 1, 9. See also Trumpism

Harper, Kyle: and Constantinianism,
    56–57; The Fate of Rome, 8, 56–59;
    and Late Antique Little Ice Age,
    56–58; and Roman climate opti-
    mum, 56
Hesiod, 3–4, 23, 42, 44
heterogeneous connections, 6–7, 13, 40,
    43, 45, 49–50, 58. See also abstract
    machine; agency; entanglement

Holland, Eugene, 100n5
Honig, Bonnie, 103n13, 103n17
horizontal gene transfer, 31–33, 82–84
human exceptionalism, 14–15, 24, 31,
    35, 39–44, 48, 60, 101–2n12; and en-
    tangled humanism, 40–44. See also
    evolution; planetary; sociocentrism

"ifs," 29–30
Ignatov, Anatoli, and perspectivalism, 105

Kant, Immanuel, 84–85, 87; and Augus-
    tine, 4, 102n2; in the major tradition,
    3–4, 11, 17, 19, 42, 87; and planetary
    gradualism, 42, 44
Keller, Catherine, 24, 41–42, 57, 59,
    104n21, 106n14

Late Antique Little Ice Age, 56–59, 65,
    106n11

major and minor tradition, 3–6, 13, 18–19,
    60–61; Deleuze and Guattari on, 6, 42,
    99–100n3, 102n4, 105n37, 112n19
Marx, Karl: in the major and minor
    tradition, 4, 6, 100n5; and Kropotkin,
    4, 100n6
Mayer, Emeran, and mind-gut connec-
    tions, 110
McCarthyism, 2
McIntyre, Lee, 100n9
media, 1, 52, 54, 62, 94
memory, below recollection, 28, 76–77
micropolitics. See activism
mimetic contagion, 100n4
minorities, 1, 13, 64, 70; minoritization, 48
misogyny, 1–2, 63
Moore, Jason, and Capitalocene, 62–65

nature, 2, 18, 35, 44, 61, 85, 87; exploi-
    tation of, 54, 63–64; human mastery
    over, 27, 35, 40–42, 74, 88; nature/
    culture division, 4–5, 29, 33, 42, 92

neoliberalism, 1–2, 9, 15, 85; Foucault on, 113n25; neoliberal capitalism, 51–55, 62. *See also* capitalism; evangelicalism

neopositivism, 10–11, 16, 101n10; Foucault and Whitehead on, 96. *See also* truth

neuroscience, 1, 83; mirror neurons, 79; neuroscientific experiments, 110n13, 111n14

New Left, 2

Nietzsche, Friedrich, 76, 91, 94; eternal return, 104n30; and Foucault, 19, 73, 89, 102n14; in the minor tradition, 3, 42, 44; and Williams, 18–19

nihilism, 71, 94, 97

Nixey, Catherine, 57, 106n14

nonhuman. *See* agency; planetary; Sophocles

ocean conveyor system, 5, 7, 37, 43, 65–66, 68–69, 93

plagues, and Rome, 55–58

planetary: amplifiers, 7–8, 23, 35, 39, 42–45, 47, 58, 61, 63, 66–71, 90–91; and efficient causality, 58; processes, 3, 5, 20, 22, 38–39, 50–51, 65, 80, 91, 97; temporality, 12, 38, 67, 69; as time machine, 6–7, 9, 50, 56, 66, 69, 70; volatility, 5–6, 8, 21–22, 24, 34, 38, 41–42, 47–48, 64, 90–91, 93, 97, 99n3, 100n4, 100n6, 105n39. *See also* abstract machine; climate change; planetary gradualism

planetary gradualism, 4–5, 10, 15, 20, 24, 46–48, 59, 62, 93, 113n24; and human exceptionalism, 6, 41–44, 91

Plato, 3, 17, 19

pluralism, 4, 10, 16, 54, 61, 106n6

pluripotentialities, 30, 32; in Whitehead, 84, 111n15. *See also* agency; "ifs"; real creativity

politics of swarming, 106n9, 108n26. *See also* activism

Pope Francis, 24, 61

postmodernism, 10–11, 100n9

precursors, 28, 37

presumptive generosity, 4, 11–12, 16

process theory, 11, 60, 78, 101n12. *See also* major and minor tradition

quantum: theory, 10, 15, 32, 77, 91–92, 112n23; world, 32, 112n20

Rawls, John, 3–4; and planetary gradualism, 42

real creativity, 11–12, 14–15, 73; Foucault on, 78; Whitehead on, 13, 81, 87, 111n16. *See also* planetary; process theory; speculative philosophy

Rome. *See* fall of Rome

scars of the past, in Whitehead, 76, 83–85, 110

Schmitt, Carl, 59–60

scientific hubris, 3, 31, 35

secularism, 46, 59–61, 76–77, 81, 95, 100n4, 103n17

self-organizing processes, 3, 5–7, 31–33, 50–51, 65, 67. *See also* abstract machine; ocean conveyor system; real creativity

Shelley, Mary, 5, 26, 38, 41, 45, 92, 95; and climate events, 3, 27, 35–38; on evolution, 30, 33–35; *Frankenstein: Prometheus Unbound*, 3, 27–30, 35–37; *The Last Man*, 93; on nature/culture distinctions, 29, 33; and planetary volatilities, 36–38

Shelley, Percy Bysshe, 26, 28, 30, 38, 92

social movements, 2, 7, 52, 62, 86, 97; as pluralist assemblages, 24, 49

sociocentrism, 5–6, 9, 38–44, 49, 92; and human exceptionalism, 39, 41–43, 90; and planetary conditions, 38, 43, 48, 91. *See also* human exceptionalism

Sophocles, 4–5, 31; *Antigone*, 21, 23; and Foucault, 79; *Oedipus at Colonus*, 20–22, 103n13; and planetary volatility, 3, 18, 20–23; and Whitehead, 93–94; in Williams, 17–20, 24. *See also* tragic vision of possibility

speculative philosophy, 4, 10–12; Erasmus Darwin and, 35; Whitehead on, 12–15, 80–82, 92, 96, 109n4, 111n14. *See also* process theory

symbiogenesis, 49, 79. *See also* bacteria

tactics/techniques of the self. *See* Foucault, Michel

temporality: heterogeneous and planetary, 11–13, 16, 37–38, 50, 69, 89–90; temporal volatilities, 20, 91

Theweleit, Klaus, 29

Thucydides: in Williams, 5, 17–20. *See also* Williams, Bernard

tragic vision of possibility, 22–23, 42, 89, 103n13; and tragedy, 89–90

transcendental arguments, 4, 18, 80, 86, 111n14, 111n15

triggers. *See* capitalism; climate change

Trump, Donald, 1, 10, 47, 55, 59, 99n1; and aspirational fascism, 2–3, 53, 60, 62; and climate denialism, 52–53. *See also* Trumpism

Trumpism, 2, 9, 106n6; and fake news, 10, 108n2

truth: coherence model of, 11, 13–14, 83; correspondence theory of, 10–12, 14, 73, 78; lure of, 13–16, 77, 86–87, 96–97; post-truth, 10, 12, 96; regimes of, 2, 4, 13–15, 77–78, 85, 87, 96–97, 101n9; will to, 73–74, 83, 86, 88, 94. *See also* Foucault, Michel; Whitehead, Alfred N.

Vidal-Naquet, Pierre, 103n13

visceral register, 76–77, 79–80

violence, as pre-accomplished, 84–85

volatility. *See* planetary; temporality

volcanic eruption, 6–7, 23, 26, 38, 43, 70; Late Antique Little Ice Age, 58; of Mount Tambora, 25–26, 35, 104n22

Weber, Max: on capitalism, 4–6; in the major tradition, 3–4, 42; and planetary gradualism, 42

West, Cornel, 25

White, Sam, 107n23

white triumphalism, 1, 52–53. *See also* Trumpism

Whitehead, Alfred N.: creative advance, 82, 89, 113n24; and Foucault, 13, 16, 72–97, 111n14; and gender duality, 77–78; horizontal evolution, 82–83; against human exceptionalism, 41, 83, 89–90; on micro-agencies, 82–83, 109n6, 110n11; lure of truth, 13, 15, 77–78, 83; against neopositivism, 101n9; and Nietzsche, 76, 109n5; panexperientialism, 102n12, 109n5, 112n20; and quantum theory, 15, 77, 112n23; real creativity, 13, 81, 83–84, 87, 111n16; and romanticism, 79, 89, 91–93, 109n7; scars of the past, 76, 83–84; and Sophocles, 93–94; on speculative and process philosophy, 12–15, 80–82, 92, 96, 102n12, 109n4, 111n14; on transcendentalism, 86, 111n14; truth as aspiration, 86–87, 96

Williams, Bernard, 3, 19–20, 39; and analytic philosophy, 17–18; and human exceptionalism, 41; on major and minor traditions, 5, 19, 42, 99n3; on Sophocles, 3, 5, 17–19, 21–22, 24, 99n3; on Thucydides, 5, 17–19, 99n3

workers, 1, 51, 53–54, 59–60, 94, 99n1; white working and lower middle class, 1, 53, 62

world of becoming, 13, 66–67, 79